THE STORY
OF
ANCIENT IRISH
CIVILISATION

BY
P. W. JOYCE

PREFACE.

This little book has been written and published with the main object of spreading as widely as possible among our people, young and old, a knowledge of the civilisation and general social condition of Ireland from the fifth or sixth to the twelfth century, when it was wholly governed by native rulers. The publication comes at an appropriate time, when there is an awakening of interest in the Irish language, and in Irish lore of every kind, unparalleled in our history.

But the book has a further mission. There are many English and many Anglo-Irish people who think, merely from ignorance, that Ireland was a barbarous and half-savage country before the English came among the people and civilised them. This book, so far as it finds its way among the two classes above mentioned, will, I fancy, open their eyes. They will learn from it that the old Irish, so far from being barbarous,[Pg vi] were a bright, intellectual, and cultured people; that they had professions, trades, and industries pervading the whole population, with clearly defined ranks and grades of society, all working under an elaborate system of native laws; and that in the steadying and civilising arts and pursuits of everyday life they were as well advanced, as orderly, and as regular as any other European people of the same period. They will find too that, as regards education, scholarship, and general mental culture, the Irish of those early ages were in advance of all other countries of Europe; that they helped most materially to spread Christianity, and to revive learning, all over the Continent; and that to Irish missionaries and scholars, the Anglo-Saxons of the Heptarchy were indebted for the greater part of their Christianity, and for the preservation and restoration of learning when it was threatened with extinction all over England by the ravages of the Danes.

But there were, and are, Englishmen better informed about our country. More than three hundred years ago the great English poet,[Pg vii] Edmund Spenser, lived for some time in Ireland, and made himself well acquainted with its history. He knew what it was in past ages; so that in one of his poems he speaks of the time

"When Ireland flourishèd in fame
Of wealth and goodnesse, far above the rest
Of all that beare the British Islands name."

But it is better not to pursue these observations farther here, as it would be only anticipating what will be found in the body of the book.

This book is the last of a series of three, of which the second is abridged from the first, and the third from both.

The First—"A Social History of Ancient Ireland" (2 vols., richly gilt, both cover and top, in 31 chapters, with 361 Illustrations)—contains a complete survey of the Social Life and Institutions of Ancient Ireland. All the important statements in it are proved home by references to authorities, and by quotations from ancient documents.

The Second—"A Smaller Social History of Ancient Ireland" (1 vol., cloth, gilt, 598 pages, in 27 chapters, with 213 Illustrations)—traverses[Pg viii] the same ground as the larger work; but, besides condensation, most of the illustrative quotations and nearly all the references to authorities are omitted.

This Third book—"The Story of Ancient Irish Civilisation"—gives in simple, plain language, an account of the condition of the country in the olden time; but as it is here to speak for itself, I need not describe it further. For all the statements it contains, full and satisfactory authorities will be found in the two larger works.

I have done my best to make all three readable and interesting, as well as instructive.

The ordinary history of our country has been written by many, and the reader has a wide choice. But in the matter of our Social History he has no choice at all. For these three books of mine have, for the first and only time, brought within the reach of the general public a knowledge of the whole social life of Ancient Ireland.

P. W. J.

Lyre-na-Grena,
February, 1907.

[Pg ix]

The old Irish writers commonly prefixed to their books or treatises a brief statement of "Place, Time, Person, and Cause." My larger Social History, following the old custom, opens with a statement of this kind, which reappears in the Preface to the Smaller Social History, and which may be appropriately repeated here:—

The Place, Time, Author, and Cause of Writing, of this book, are:—Its place is Lyre-na-Grena, Leinster-road, Rathmines, Dublin; its time is the year of our Lord one thousand nine hundred and seven; the author is Patrick Weston Joyce, Doctor of Laws; and the cause of writing the same book is to give glory to God, honour to Ireland, and knowledge to those who desire to learn all about the Old Irish People.

ANCIENT IRISH CIVILISATION.

CHAPTER I.

HOW THE ANCIENT IRISH PEOPLE WERE GOVERNED BY THEIR KINGS AND CHIEFS.

There were in Ireland, from times beyond the reach of history, kings, who were of various grades according to the extent of the country or district they ruled over. The highest of all was the king of Ireland, who lived in the royal palace at Tara. He was called the Ard-ri [ard-ree], *i.e.*, 'High king' or Over-king, because he claimed authority over all the others. There was also a king over each of the five provinces—Leinster, Munster, Connaught, Ulster, and Meath—who were subject to the Ard-ri. The provinces were divided into a number of territories, over which were kings of a still lower grade, each under the king of his own province. If the district was not large enough to have a king, it was ruled by a chief, who was subject to the king of the larger territory in which the district was included.

[Pg 2]The king was always chosen from one particular ruling family; and when a king died, those chiefs who had votes held a meeting, lasting for three days and three nights, at which they elected whatever member of that family they considered the wisest, best, and bravest. After this a day was fixed for inaugurating the new king, a ceremony corresponding in some respects with the *crowning* of our present monarchs. This Inauguration, or 'making' of a king as it is called in Irish, was a great affair, and was attended by all the leading people, both clergymen and laymen. There was always one particular spot for the ceremony, on which usually stood a high mound or fort, with an 'Inauguration Stone' on top, and often a great branching old tree, under the shade of which the main proceedings were carried on.

The new king, standing on the Inauguration Stone, swore a solemn oath in the hearing of all, that he would govern his people with strict justice, and that he would observe the laws of the land, and maintain the old customs of the tribe or kingdom. Then he put by his sword; and one of the chiefs, whose special office it was, put into his hand a long, straight, white wand. This was to signify that he was to govern, not[Pg 3] by violence or harshness, but by justice, and that his decisions were to be straight and stainless like the wand. Several other forms had to be gone through till the ceremony was completed; and he was then the lawful king.

The old Irish kings lived in great style, especially those of the higher ranks, and—like the kings of our own day—kept in their palaces numbers of persons to attend on them, holding various offices, all with good salaries. The higher the grade of the king the greater the number of his household, and the grander the persons holding offices. Forming part of his retinue there were nobles, who did nothing at all but wait on him, merely to do him honour. There were *Ollaves*, i.e., learned and distinguished men, of the several professions— Historians, Poets, Physicians, Builders, Brehons or Judges, Musicians, and so forth. All were held in high honour, and exercised their several professions for the benefit of the king and his household, for which each had a house and a tract of land free, or some other equivalent stipend.

Then there was a house-steward, who issued orders each day for the provisions to be laid in for next day—the number of oxen, sheep, and hogs to be slaughtered, the quantity of bread to be baked,[Pg 4]and of ale, mead, and wine to be measured out; and he regulated the reception of guests, their arrangement at banquets, and their sleeping accommodation; with numerous other matters of a like kind, all pertaining to the household. His word was law,

2

and no one ever thought of questioning his arrangements. The house-steward's office was one of great responsibility, and he had plenty of anxiety and worry; and accordingly he held a high rank, and was well paid for his services.

There was a champion—a fierce and mighty man—who answered challenges, and, when necessary, fought single combats for the honour of the king. Guards were always at hand, who remained standing up with drawn swords or battleaxes during dinner. There was a master of horse, with numerous grooms; keepers of the king's jewels and chessboards; couriers or runners to convey the king's messages and orders, and to bring him tidings; keepers of hounds and coursing dogs; a chief swineherd, with his underlings; fools, jugglers, and jesters for the amusement of the company; with a whole army of under-servants and workmen of various kinds.

Each day the whole company sat in the great hall at dinner, arranged at tables in the order of rank the great grandees and the ollaves near the[Pg 5] king, others of less importance lower down, while the attendants—when they were not otherwise occupied—sat at tables of their own at the lower end of the hall. To pay the expenses of his great household, and to enable him to live in grandeur as a king should live, he had a large tract of land free, besides which, every tenant and householder throughout his dominion had to make a yearly payment according to his means. These payments were made, not in money—for there was little or no coined money then—but *in kind*; that is to say, cattle and provisions of various sorts, plough-oxen, hogs, sheep, with mantles and other articles of dress; also dyestuffs, sewing-thread, firewood, horses, rich bridles, chessboards, jewellery, and sometimes gold and silver reckoned out in ounces, as Abraham paid Ephron for the cave of Machpelah. Much income also accrued to the king from other sources not mentioned here; and he wanted it all, for he was expected to be lavish in giving presents, and hospitable without stint in receiving and entertaining guests.

Besides all this, the king often went on what was called a 'Free Circuit,' *i.e.*, a visitation through his dominions, moving quite leisurely in his chariot from place to place, with a numerous retinue, all in their own chariots; while the[Pg 6] several sub-kings through whose territories he passed had to lodge, feed, and entertain the whole company free, while they remained.

These old Irish kings—when they were not engaged in war—seem to have led a free and easy life, and to have had a pleasanter time of it than the kings and emperors of our own day.

The Irish took care that their kings had not too much power in their hands; so that they could not always do as they pleased—a proper and wise arrangement. They were what we now call 'limited monarchs'; that is, they could not enter on any important undertaking affecting the kingdom or the public without consulting their people. On such occasions the king had to call a meeting of his chief men, and ask their advice, and, if necessary, take their votes when there was a difference of opinions. And besides this, kings, as we shall see farther on, had to obey the law the same as their subjects.

Each king, of whatever grade, should, according to law, have at least three chief residences; and he lived in them by turns, as suited his fancy or convenience. Nearly all those old palaces are known at the present day; and in most of them the ramparts and mounds are still to be seen, more[Pg 7] or less dilapidated after the long lapse of time. The ruins of the most important ones—such as we see them now—are described in some detail in my two Social Histories of Ancient Ireland; but here our space will not permit us to mention more than a few.

The most important of all is Tara, the chief residence of the over-kings, which is situated on the summit of a gentle green hill, six miles from Navan in Meath, and two miles from the Midland Railway station of Kilmessan. The various mounds, circular ramparts, and other features are plainly marked on the plan given at the beginning of this book; and anyone who walks over the hill with the plan in his hand can easily recognise them.

Next to Tara in celebrity was the palace of Emain or Emania, the residence of the kings of Ulster, and the chief home of Concobar Mac Nessa and the Red Branch Knights. The imposing remains of this palace, consisting of a great mound surrounded by an immense circular rampart and fosse half obliterated, the whole structure covering about eleven English acres, lie two miles west of Armagh.

Another Ulster palace, quite as important as Emain, was Ailech, the ruins of which are situated[Pg 8] in County Donegal, on the summit of a hill 800 feet high, five miles north-west from Derry. It is a circular stone fortress of dry masonry, still retaining its old name in the form of "Greenan-Ely."

The chief palace of the kings of Connaught was Croghan, the old fort of which lies three miles from Tulsk in Roscommon.

The most important residence of the Leinster kings was Aillenn, now called Knockaulin, an immense fort surrounding the summit of a hill near Kilcullen in Kildare.

Besides these there are the Munster palaces, the Rock of Cashel, Kincora at Killaloe, Bruree in Limerick, and Caher in Tipperary: also we have Naas in Kildare, Dunlavin in Wicklow, Dinnree in Carlow, and many others.

CHAPTER II.

HOW THE WARLIKE OLD IRISH CONQUERED FOREIGN LANDS.

From the remotest times the Irish had a genius for war and a love of fighting; and if it fell within the scope of this narrative, it would be easy to show that these features in our character have[Pg 9] come down to the present day. For good or for bad, we are, and always have been, a fighting race.

In old times the 'Scots'—as the Irish were then called—were well known for their warlike qualities, and very much dreaded; so that fabulous rumours regarding them ran among some of the people of the Continent. One Latin writer tells us that Irish mothers were wont to present the first food on the point of a sword to their newly-born male infants, as a sort of dedication to war. This is certainly an invention, for it is not mentioned in our own records; but it indicates the character the Irish people had earned for themselves abroad. They fought a great deal too much among themselves at home; but in this respect they were not a bit worse than the English people at the time of the Heptarchy or than the Continental nations of the same period.

That the old Irish should be warlike is only what we might expect; seeing that they were in great measure descended from the Continental Gauls, who in ancient times were renowned as warriors and conquerors. But mighty as the Gauls were, and though they were at least as brave as the Romans, they were subdued in the end by superior discipline, when Julius Cæsar[Pg 10] invaded them. And so with the old Irish. Though they were fierce and strong, and taken man for man quite a match for the Anglo-Normans, they were forced, after a long struggle, to yield to science, skill, and discipline, when they were invaded by that people—then the greatest warriors in the world.

The Irish were not content with fighting at home, but made themselves formidable in foreign lands. Their chief foreign conquests were in Wales and Scotland; but they frequently found their way to the Continent. Irish literature of every kind abounds in records of foreign raids, invasions, and inter-marriages; and in many particulars these native accounts are borne out by authorities that no one questions, namely, Roman classical writers, whenever they find occasion to touch on these matters.

Those who have read the early history of England will remember that the Picts and Scots, marching southwards from the Scottish Highlands, gave much trouble, year after year, for a long period, to the Romans and Britons. The Picts were the people of Scotland at the time; and the Scots were the Irish, who, crossing over to Alban or Scotland in their *currągh* fleets, joined the Picts in their formidable raids southwards.[Pg 11] We know all this, not only from our own native historians, but also from Roman writers, who tell us how the Romans had often to fight in Britain against the Scots from Ireland.

In order to protect the British people against these two fierce nations, the Romans, at different intervals in the second and third centuries, built great walls or ramparts from sea to sea, between Britain and Alban, of which the ruins are still to be seen: one beginning at the Frith of Clyde and another at the Solway Frith.

For several hundred years—from the third to the sixth century, and even after—the Irish streamed continually to Scotland across the narrow sea. The first of these migrations of which we have reliable accounts originated in a famine, exactly as the great exodus of our own day from Ireland to America was set going by the terrible famine of 1847. And this migration is related partly by old Irish writers, and partly by the great English historian, the Venerable Bede.

The famine in question fell on Munster early in the third century, so that numbers of people were forced to leave the province. One particular chief led a great host of fighting men, with their families, northwards, till they reached the extreme[Pg 12] district now known as the county Antrim. Here they divided: and while one part remained in Ireland (i.e., in Antrim), the other part, under the same leader mentioned above, crossed over to Alban or Scotland, where they settled down. From this time forward, there was a continual migration, year after year, from the northern coast to Scotland, till, after the lapse of about three centuries, occurred the greatest invasion of all, led by the three brothers, Fergus, Angus, and Lorne, in the year 503.

It has been already related in our Histories of Ireland, and need not be repeated in detail here, how these colonists ultimately mastered the country, over which their first king, Fergus, ruled; how they gave Scotland its name; how the subsequent kings of Scotland were the direct descendants of Fergus; and how from him again, through the Stuarts, descend, in one of their lines of pedigree, our present royal family.

At about the same period the Irish mastered and peopled the Isle of Man; and for centuries there was constant intercourse between the parent people of the north-east coast of Ireland and this little colony. Though the Norsemen wrested the sovereignty of the island from them in the ninth century, they did not succeed in[Pg 13] displacing either the Gaelic people or their language. The best possible proof that the Irish colonised and held possession of Man for ages is the fact that the Manx language is nothing more than Irish Gaelic, slightly changed by lapse of time. There are also still to be seen all over the island Irish buildings and monuments, mixed up, however, with many of Norse origin; and the great majority of both the place-names and the native family-names are Gaelic.

In our old historical books we have accounts of migrations of Irish people to Wales, some as invaders intending to return, some as colonists purposing to settle and remain. At this time the Romans were masters of England and Wales, but they were not as mighty a people in the fourth century as they had been previously; for on the Continent the northern barbarians were pressing on them everywhere; and in Britain the Picts and Scots, as we have said, kept continually harassing them from the north.

These raids became at last so intolerable, that the Roman government sent an able general named Theodosius (father of the emperor Theodosius the Great) to Britain to check them. At the very time that Theodosius was in Britain, a brave and strong-handed king reigned in Tara,[Pg 14] named Criffan (A.D., 366 to 379), who on several occasions invaded Britain, and took possession of large tracts, so that he is called in our old records "Criffan the Great, king of Ireland, and of Albion to the British Channel." The Roman historians tell us that Theodosius succeeded in beating back the Picts and Scots, and even chased them out to sea, in which there is probably some exaggeration, as there is, no doubt, on the part of our own historians in calling Criffan "King of Albion to the British Channel."

Criffan was succeeded by Niall of the Nine Hostages (A.D. 379 to 405), who was still more distinguished for foreign conquests than his predecessor. He invaded Britain on a more extensive and formidable scale than had yet been attempted, and swept over a large extent of country, bringing away immense booty and whole crowds of captives, but was at length forced to retreat by the valiant Roman general Stilicho. On this occasion a Roman poet, praising Stilicho, says of him—speaking as Britannia:—"By him was I protected when the Scot [i.e., Niall] moved all Ireland against me, and the ocean foamed with their hostile oars."

For the extensive scale of these terrible raids we have the testimony of the best possible[Pg 15] authority—St. Patrick—who, in his "Confession," speaking of the expedition in which he himself was taken captive (probably that led by Niall), says:—"I was

5

about sixteen years of age, when I was brought captive into Ireland *with many thousand persons.*"

The preceding were warlike raids; but no doubt, while the main body of the host returned on each occasion to their homes in Ireland, large numbers remained and settled down in Wales. But we have an account of at least one expedition undertaken with the direct object of colonising. In the third century, a powerful tribe called the Desii, who occupied the territory of *Deece*, near Tara, were expelled from the district by King Cormac Mac Art, for a serious breach of law. Part of these went to Munster, and settled in a territory which still bears their name, the barony of Decies, in Waterford. Another part, crossing over to Wales under one of their leaders, took possession of a district called Dyfed, where they settled down and kept themselves distinct as an immigrant tribe, speaking their own language for generations, till at length they were absorbed by the more numerous population around them, just as, many centuries later, the Anglo-Normans who came to Ireland were absorbed by the Irish.

[Pg 16]We are told in Cormac's Glossary that in those times it was quite a usual thing for Irish chiefs to own two territories, one in Ireland and the other in Wales; and that they visited and lived in each by turns, as suited their convenience or pleasure. And the Irish chiefs often crossed over to receive the tributes due to them from their Welsh possessions.

Plain marks and tokens of these migrations and settlements exist in Wales at the present day, as we are told by eminent Welsh writers who have examined the question. Numerous places are still called after Irishmen, as, for instance, Holyhead, of which the Welsh name means the 'Rocks of the Gaels.' The Irish, wherever they settled down in Wales, built for themselves circular forts, as was their custom at home in Ireland. Many of these remain to this day, and are called 'Irishmen's Cottages.' Moreover, the present spoken Welsh language contains a number of Irish words, borrowed by the people from their Irish neighbours in days of old. All this we are told—as already stated—by several great Welsh scholars.

[Pg 17]
CHAPTER III.
HOW KINGS, CHIEFS, AND PEOPLE WERE SUBJECT TO THE BREHON LAWS.

The ancient Irish had a system of laws which grew up gradually among them from time immemorial. And there were lawyers who made law the business of their lives, and lived by it. When a lawyer was very distinguished, and became noted for his knowledge, skill, and justice, he was recognised as competent to act as a *Brehon* or judge. A brehon was also a magistrate by virtue of his position. From this word 'brehon,' the old Irish law is now commonly called the 'Brehon Law.'

We have seen that every king kept in his household distinguished men of all the learned professions, and paid them well. Among these the brehon always held a high place; so that a large number of brehons found employment in this way. But many were unattached, and lived by deciding cases brought before them; for which they held courts, and were paid fees by the litigants in each case. On these fees they lived,[Pg 18] for they had no regular salaries. And there were practising lawyers also, not holding the position of brehon, who made a living by their profession, like lawyers of our day.

To become a lawyer a person had to go through a regular course of study and training. The subjects were laid down with great exactness from year to year of the course; and the time was much longer than that required by a young man now-a-days to become a barrister. Until the student had put in the full time, and mastered the whole course, he was not permitted to practise as a lawyer of any kind—pleader, law-agent, professor of law, law-adviser, or brehon.

Law was perhaps the most difficult of all the professions to study. For there were many strange terms hard to understand, all of which had to be learned, many puzzling forms to be gone through, many circumstances to be taken into account in all transactions where law was brought in, or where trials took place in a brehon's court. And if there was the least flaw or omission, if the smallest error was committed, either by the client or by his lawyer, it was instantly pounced upon by the opposing pleader, and the case was likely enough to go against them.

[Pg 19]As soon as the Irish had learned the art of writing, they began to write down their laws in books. There is the best reason to believe that before the time of St. Patrick the pagan brehons had law-books. But they were full of paganism—pagan gods, pagan customs, and pagan expressions everywhere through them; and they would not answer for a Christian people. So about six years after St. Patrick's arrival, when Christianity had been pretty widely spread through Ireland, he saw that it was necessary to have a new code, suitable for the new and pure faith; and he advised Laeghaire [Laery], the ard-ri, to take steps to have the laws revised and re-written. The king, seeing this could not be avoided, appointed nine learned and eminent persons—of whom he himself and St. Patrick were two—to carry out this important work. At the end of three years, these nine produced a new code, quite free from any taint of paganism: and this book got the name of Senchus Mór [Shannahus More], meaning 'Great old law-book.'

The very book left by St. Patrick and the others has been long lost. But successive copies were made from time to time, of which some are still preserved. We have also manuscript copies[Pg 20] of several other old Irish law-books, most of which, as well as the Senchus Mór, have been lately translated and printed. As the language of those old books is very obscure and difficult, it was a hard task to translate them; but this was successfully done by the two great Irish scholars, Dr. John O'Donovan and Professor Eugene O'Curry. These translations of the Senchus Mór and the other old law-books, with the Irish texts, and with notes, explanations, and indexes, form six large printed volumes, which may now be seen in every important library.

The brehons held courts at regular intervals, where cases were tried. If a man was wronged by another, he summoned him to one of these courts, and there were lawyers to plead for both sides, and witnesses were examined, much in the same way as we see in our present law courts; and after the brehon had carefully listened to all, he gave his decision. This decision was given by the brehon alone: there were no juries such as we have now.

All parties, high and low, submitted to the Brehon Laws, and abided by the judge's decisions; unless the party who lost the suit thought the decision wrong—which indeed happened but seldom—in which case, he appealed to the court of a[Pg 21] higher brehon. Then, if it was found that the first had given an unjust decision, he had to return the fee and pay damages, besides more or less losing character, and lessening his chances of further employment. So the brehons had to be very careful in trying cases and giving their decisions.

The highest people in the land, even kings and queens, had to submit to the laws, exactly the same as common subjects; and if a king was wronged, he had to appeal to the law, like other people. A couple of hundred years ago, when the kings of France were, to all intents and purposes, despotic, and could act much as they pleased towards their subjects, a learned French writer on law, during a visit to England, happened to pass near the grounds of one of the palaces, where he observed a notice on the fence of a field belonging to the king:—"Trespassers will be prosecuted according to law." Now this gave him great pleasure, as it showed how the king had to call in the aid of the law to redress a wrong, like any of his subjects; and it gave him occasion to contrast the condition of England with that of France, where the king or queen would have made short work of the trespasser, without any notice or law at all.

[Pg 22]But if the same Frenchman had been in Ireland 1,500 years ago, he might have witnessed what would give him still greater pleasure:—not a mere notice, but an actual case of trespass on a queen's ground, tried in open court before his eyes. In those days there reigned at Tara a king named Mac Con, whose queen had a plot of land, not far from the palace, planted with *glasheen*, i.e., the woad-plant, for dyeing blue. In the neighbourhood there lived a female *brewy*, or keeper of a hostel for travellers, who had flocks and herds like all other brewys. One night a flock of sheep belonging to her broke into the queen's grounds, and ate up or destroyed the whole crop of glasheen; whereupon the queen summoned her for damages.

7

In due course the case came before the king (for the queen would not appear before an ordinary brehon), and on hearing the evidence he decided that the sheep should be forfeit to the queen to pay for the crop. Now, although the glasheen was an expensive and valuable crop, the sheep were worth a great deal more; and the people were enraged at this unjust sentence; but they dared not speak out, for Mac Con was a usurper and a tyrant.

Among the people who dwelt in Tara at this time[Pg 23] was a boy, a handsome, noble-looking young fellow, whom the people all knew by the name of Cormac. But no one in the least suspected that he was in reality a prince, the son of the last monarch, Art the Solitary, who had been slain in battle by the usurper, Mac Con. He was wise and silent, and carefully concealed from all who he was; for he well knew that if he was discovered the king would be sure to kill him.

While the trial was going on he stood behind the crowd listening quietly; and being by nature noble and just-minded, even from his youth up, he could not contain himself when he heard the king's unfair and oppressive sentence; and he cried out amid the dead silence:—"That is an unjust judgment! Let the fleeces be given up for the glasheen—the sheep-crop for the land-crop—for both will grow again!"

The king was astonished and enraged, and became still more so when the people exclaimed with one voice:—"That is a true judgment, and he who has pronounced it is surely the son of a king!"

In this manner the people, to their great joy, discovered who Cormac was. How he managed to escape the vengeance of the king we are not told; but escape he did; and after a time the usurper was expelled from Tara, and Cormac was[Pg 24] put in his place. To this day Cormac Mac Art is celebrated in Irish records as a skilful lawyer and writer on law, and as the wisest and most illustrious of all the ancient Irish kings.[1]

CHAPTER IV.
HOW THE ANCIENT IRISH LIVED AS PAGANS.

When Ireland was pagan the people were taught their religion, such as it was, by Druids. These druids were the only learned men of the time, and they had in their hands all the learned professions—they were not only druids, but judges, prophets, poets, and even physicians. They were the only teachers, and they were employed to instruct the sons and daughters of kings and chiefs in whatever learning was then known. They were also advisers to king and people on all important occasions; so they were, as we can well understand, held in high estimation, and had great[Pg 25] influence. They had the reputation of being mighty magicians, and could do many wonderful things, as our old romantic stories tell, and as the people firmly believed. They could raise a druidical or magic fog, which hid things from view, or bring on darkness in the day, like the blackest night; they could bring down showers of fire or blood, cause a snowfall even in summer, till the ground was covered half a yard deep; and bring on storms and tempests on sea or land. They could drive a man mad by their sorcery—a power which was dreaded most of all by the people in general. For this purpose the druid prepared what was called a 'madman's wisp,' that is, a little wisp of straw or grass, into which he pronounced some foul, baleful verses; and, watching his opportunity, he flung it into the face of the poor victim, who straightway became a madman, or, what was just as bad, an idiot—all beyond cure. Many other instances of the power of their spells are related in old Irish tales.

They were often employed in divination, i.e., foretelling the future. Sometimes they forecasted by observing the clouds or the stars, sometimes by means of a rod of yew with Ogham letters cut upon it, often by interpreting dreams, or from sneezing, or by the voices of birds, especially the[Pg 26] croaking of the raven, or the chirping of the wren. By some or all of these means they professed to be able to tell the issue of a coming battle, or whether a man's life was to be long or short, and what were the lucky or unlucky days for beginning any work, or for undertaking any enterprise; besides many other matters lying in the future.

The Greeks and Romans of old had—as we know—their augurs or soothsayers, who forecasted the future, like our druids, and by much the same observations, signs, and tokens.

We must not judge those old people, whether Greek, Roman, or Irish, too severely for believing in these prophets; for although there are no druids or soothsayers now, we have amongst us plenty of palmists and fortune-tellers of various kinds, who make a good living out of those people who are simple enough to believe in them.

There were druids in every part of Ireland; but Tara, as being the residence of the over-kings, was their chief seat, where they were most powerful; and those who have read the early history of Ireland will recollect St. Patrick's contest with them, in presence of king Laeghaire [Laery] and his court, and how he put them down in argument.

[Pg 27]The pagan Irish had many gods and many idols. Among other things, they worshipped the Fairies, who were, and are still, called in Irish *Shee*. The fairies dwelt under pleasant green little hills; and there they built themselves palaces all ablaze with light, and glittering with gems and gold. These residences, as well as the elves or fairies themselves, were called *Shee*. Many of the old fairy hills all over the country are still well known; and to this day there is a superstition among many of the people that the fairies still remain in them, and that they also dwell in the old *lisses, raths,* or forts that are found everywhere in Ireland. The fairies were not always confined to their dwellings: they often got out, but they were generally invisible. Whenever they made themselves visible to mortals—and that was only seldom—they were seen to be very small, hardly the height of a man's knee. People had to be careful of them, for they often did mischief when interfered with.

Mannanan Mac Lir was the Irish sea-god, like Neptune of the Greeks and Romans. He generally lived on the sea, riding in his chariot at the head of his followers. He is in his glory on a stormy night, and on such a night, when you look over the waste of waters, there before your eyes, in the dim[Pg 28] gloom, are thousands of Mannanan's white steeds careering along after their great chief's chariot.

Angus Mac-an-oge was a mighty magician, who had his glorious palace under the great mound of Brugh [Broo] on the Boyne, now called Newgrange, a little below Slane in Meath. There were many other gods; and there were goddesses also. Poets, physicians, and smiths had three goddesses whom they severally worshipped, three sisters, all named Brigit. There were also many fairy queens, who were considered as goddesses and worshipped in their several districts, all living in their palaces under fairy mounds or rocks.

Many of these residences are still well known, such as Carrigcleena, a circle of grey rocks near Mallow, where lived Cleena, the fairy queen of south Munster; and Craglea, near Killaloe, where Eevin or Eevil, the guardian fairy queen of the Dalcassians of Thomond, resided. The people of several districts had local gods also, such as Donn, the king of the Munster fairies, who had his airy home on the top of Knockfierna, near Croom in Limerick; John Macananty of Scrabo carn, near Newtownards; and Tierna, the powerful and kindly fairy lord, who lived in his bright palace under the great carn on the hill of Carntierna, over Fermoy.

[Pg 29]Besides those that were acknowledged and worshipped as gods or goddesses, there were battle-furies who delighted in blood and slaughter; also loathsome-looking witch-hags, and plenty of goblins, sprites, and spectres—some harmless, some malignant—who will be found enumerated and described in either of my two Social Histories.

The idols worshipped by the pagan Irish were nearly all of them stones, mostly pillar-stones, which were sometimes covered over with gold, silver, or bronze. The people also worshipped the elements—that is to say, water, fire, the sun, the wind, and such like. The worship of wells was very general. Most of those old Pagan fountains were taken possession of by St. Patrick, St. Columkille, and other early missionaries, who blessed them, and devoted them to baptism and other Christian uses; so that they came to be called holy wells; and though they were no longer worshipped, they were as much venerated by the Christians as they had been by the pagans.

It must not be supposed that each of the objects mentioned above was worshipped by all the people of Ireland. Each person, in fact, worshipped whichever he pleased. And it was usual for individuals, or a tribe, to choose some[Pg 30] idol, or element, or pagan divinity, which they held in veneration as their special guardian god.

There was a belief in a pagan heaven, a land of everlasting youth, peace, and happiness, beautiful beyond conception, called by various names, such as Teernanoge, Moy

Mell, I-Brassil, etc., which is often described as being situated far out in the Western Ocean. It was inhabited by fairies, but it was not for human beings, except a few individuals who were brought thither by the fairies.

There is a pretty story, more than a thousand years old, in the Book of the Dun Cow, which tells how Prince Connla of the Golden Hair, son of the great king Conn the Hundred-Fighter, was carried off by a fairy in a crystal boat to Moy-Mell. One day—as the story relates—while the king and Connla, and many nobles were standing on the western sea-shore, a boat of shining crystal was seen moving towards them: and when it had touched the land, a fairy, like a human being, and richly dressed, came forth from it, and addressing Connla, tried to entice him into it. No one saw this strange being save Connla alone, though all heard the conversation: and the king and the nobles marvelled, and were greatly troubled. At last the fairy chanted the following words in a very sweet voice: and the moment the chant was[Pg 31] ended, the poor young prince stepped into the crystal boat, which in a moment glided swiftly away to the west: and Prince Connla was never again seen in his native land.

THE FAIRY MAIDEN'S CHANT TO PRINCE CONNLA.

I.

A land of youth, a land of rest,
A land from sorrow free;
It lies far off in the golden west,
On the verge of the azure sea.
A swift canoe of crystal bright,
That never met mortal view—
We shall reach the land ere fall of night,
In that strong and swift canoe:
We shall reach the strand
Of that sunny land,
From druids and demons free;
The land of rest,
In the golden west,
On the verge of the azure sea!

II.

A pleasant land of winding vales, bright streams, and verdurous plains,
Where summer all the live-long year, in changeless splendour reigns;
A peaceful land of calm delight, of everlasting bloom;
Old age and death we never know, no sickness, care, or gloom;
The land of youth,
Of love and truth,
From pain and sorrow free;
The land of rest,
In the golden west,
On the verge of the azure sea!

[Pg 32]III.

There are strange delights for mortal men in that island of the west;
The sun comes down each evening in its lovely vales to rest:
And though far and dim
On the ocean's rim
It seems to mortal view,
We shall reach its halls
Ere the evening falls,
In my strong and swift canoe:
And evermore
That verdant shore

Our happy home shall be;
The land of rest,
In the golden west,
On the verge of the azure sea!

IV.

It will guard thee, gentle Connla, of the flowing golden hair;
It will guard thee from the druids, from the demons of the air;
My crystal boat will guard thee, till we reach that western shore,
Where thou and I in joy and love shall live for evermore:
From the druid's incantation,
From his black and deadly snare,
From the withering imprecation
Of the demon of the air,
It will guard thee, gentle Connla, of the flowing golden hair:
My crystal boat will guard thee, till we reach that silver strand
Where thou shalt reign in endless joy, the king of the Fairy-land![2]

[Pg 33]
CHAPTER V.
HOW THE IRISH PEOPLE LIVED AS CHRISTIANS.

It is not our business here to tell how the Irish were converted to Christianity; for this has been already related in our Histories of Ireland. Whether St. Patrick was born in Gaul or in Scotland, we know at any rate that he brought with him to Ireland, to aid him in his great work, a number of young Gauls and Britons whom he had ordained as priests. But soon after his arrival he began to ordain natives also, whom he had converted; so that the hard work of travelling through the country, and preaching to the people, was for some time in the beginning done by foreigners and Irishmen. But as time went on the missionaries were chiefly native-born. St. Patrick loved the Irish people; and he was continually praying that God would bestow favours on them. And his prayers were answered; for, after the Apostolic times, there never were more devoted or more successful missionaries than those who preached the Gospel in Ireland, and there never were people who received the[Pg 34] Faith more readily than the Irish, or who practised it after their conversion with more piety and earnestness.

An old Irish writer who lived about twelve hundred years ago tells us that the saints of Ireland who lived, and worked, and died before his time were of "Three Orders." "The First Order of Catholic saints"—says this writer—"were MOST HOLY: shining like the sun." They were 350 in number, all bishops, beginning with St. Patrick. For more than thirty years they were led by their great master, with all his fiery and tireless energy; and the preachers of this order continued for a little more than a century. They devoted themselves entirely to the home mission—the conversion of the Irish people—which gave them quite enough to do.

"The Second Order was of Catholic Priests"—continues the old writer—"numbering 300, of whom a few were bishops. These were VERY HOLY, and they shone like the moon." They lasted for a little more than half a century.

The priests of this Second Order were chiefly monastic clergy—that is to say, monks—and during their continuance monasteries were founded everywhere through Ireland. Though there were monks and monasteries here from the time of[Pg 35] St. Patrick, they began to spread much more rapidly after the foundation of the great monastery of Clonard in Meath, by St. Finnen or Finnian—one of the Second Order of saints—about the year 527. It was the monks belonging to this Order, and their successors, who preached the Gospel in foreign lands with such amazing success, as will be told in Chapter VII.

The monks and students in these establishments led a busy and happy life; for it was a rule that there should be no idleness. Everyone was to be engaged at all available times in some useful work. Some tilled the land around and belonging to the monastery—ploughing, digging, sowing, reaping—and attended to the cattle; some worked as carpenters, tailors, smiths, shoemakers, cooks, and so forth, for the use of the community. Some were set apart to receive and attend to travellers and guests, who were continually coming and going: to wash their feet, and prepare supper and bed for them. Many were employed as scribes, to copy and ornament manuscript books; while others made beautiful crosiers, brooches, chalices, crosses, and other works of metallic art; and the most scholarly members were selected to teach in the schools. Besides this, all had their devotions to attend to, which were frequent and often long.

[Pg 36]The Third Order of Irish saints consisted of about 100 priests, of whom a few were bishops: "these were HOLY, and shone like the stars"; and they lasted a little more than three-quarters of a century. They were all hermits, living either singly or in monasteries in remote lonely places. Even when they lived together in numbers they were still hermits, spending their time in prayer and contemplation, each in his own little cell; and they never met together, or had any communication with each other, except at stated times, when all assembled in the little church for common worship, or in the refectory for meals.

We know that there were nuns and convents in Ireland from St. Patrick's time, but they increased and multiplied, and flourished more than ever during and after the time of the greatest nun of all—St. Brigit of Kildare.

In the time of St. Patrick, and for long afterwards, the churches were small, because the congregations were small; and they were mostly of wood, though some were of stone. We have, in fact, the ruins of little stone-and-mortar churches still remaining in many parts of the country, built at various times during the four or five centuries after St. Patrick. In the eleventh[Pg 37] and following centuries, however, large and grand churches were built, the ruins of which still remain all over the country.

Near many of the monasteries the monks began to erect tall Round Towers in the beginning of the ninth century, as a protection against the Danes. They were built with several stories, each story lighted by one little window, and reached by a ladder inside. The door was small, and was usually ten or twelve feet from the ground. The moment word was brought that a party of Danish marauders were approaching, the monks took refuge in the tower with all their valuables and a good supply of large stones, and barred the door and windows strongly on the inside, so that it was impossible to get at them during the short time the robbers were able to stay. In fact the Danes were generally afraid of their lives to approach too close to these towers; for if one of them ventured near enough, a big stone, dropped by one of the monks from a height of sixty or seventy feet, was likely enough to come down right on his skull and make short work of him. We have still remaining many of these old towers.

There was a spring well beside every monastery, either that, or a stream of pure water. The[Pg 38] founder never selected a site till he had first ascertained that a well or a stream was near. These fountains served the double purpose of baptising converts and of supplying the communities with water. In most cases they were named after the founders, and retain their names to this day. It has been already stated how the early missionaries often took over the wells the pagans had worshipped as gods, and devoted them to Christian uses.

We have now Holy Wells in every part of Ireland, and it is with good reason we call them so, for they preserve the memory, and in most cases the very names, of those noble old missionaries who used the crystal water to baptise their converts. We ought to make it a point, so far as lies in our power, to take care of these holy wells, and to keep them neat and clean, and in all respects in a becoming condition; and also to preserve their old names as our fathers handed them down to us. If there could be such a thing as grief in heaven, an old Irish missionary would certainly feel grieved to look down on the little well he loved, and used, and blessed, now lying unnoticed and neglected.

St. Patrick used consecrated bells in celebrating the Divine Mysteries, and in nearly all other[Pg 39] religious ceremonies, and the custom has descended through fifteen centuries to this day. The bells used by the early saints were small handbells, made of iron dipped in melted bronze; but three or four hundred years after St. Patrick's time people began to make them of a better material—bronze melted and cast in moulds. We are told that St. Patrick left a little iron bell in every church he founded; and, to supply the great number he required for this purpose, he kept in his household three smiths whose sole business from morning till night was to make iron bells. The very bell he himself used in his ministrations—commonly called "The Bell of the Will"—may now be seen in the National Museum in Dublin—the most venerable of all our early Christian relics. Beside it in the same glass-case stands a beautiful and costly shrine, made by an accomplished Irish artist about the year 1100, to cover and protect it, by order and at the expense of Donall O'Loghlin, king of Ireland.

It was usual for the founders of churches to plant trees round the buildings. These "Sacred Groves," as they were called, were subsequently held in great veneration, and it was regarded as a desecration to cut down one of the trees, or even to lop off a branch.

CHAPTER VI.
HOW IRELAND BECAME THE MOST LEARNED COUNTRY IN EUROPE.
In old pagan times, long before the arrival of St. Patrick, there were schools in Ireland taught by druids. And when at last Christianity came, and was spreading rapidly over the land, those old schools were still held on; but they were no longer taught by druids, and they were no longer pagan, for teachers and scholars were now all Christians.

But as soon as St. Patrick came, a new class of schools began to spring up; for he and the other early missionaries founded monasteries everywhere through the country, and in connexion with almost every monastery there was a school. These were what are called monastic or ecclesiastical schools, for they were mostly taught by monks; while the older schools, being taught by laymen, were called lay schools.

In lay schools was taught what might be called the native learning—the learning that had grown up in the country in the course of ages. It consisted mainly of the following subjects:—To read and write the Irish language; Irish[Pg 41] grammar, and rules of poetical composition—a very extensive and complicated subject; geography and history, especially the topography and history of Ireland; and a knowledge of the poetry, and of the historical and romantic tales of the country: while a great many of the schools were for professions—special schools of law, of medicine, of poetry, of history and antiquities, and so forth. In these last the professional men were educated.

These lay schools, being now within the Christian communion, were not abolished or discouraged in any way by St. Patrick or his successors. They were simply let alone, to teach their own secular learning just as they pleased. They continued on, and were to be found in every part of Ireland for fourteen centuries after St. Patrick's arrival, down to a period within our own memory; but of course greatly changed as time went on. In later times they were much more numerous in Munster than in the other provinces; and they taught—and taught well—classics and mathematics; and often both combined in the same school. I was myself educated in some of those lay schools; and I remember with pleasure several of my old teachers: rough and unpolished men most of[Pg 42] them, but excellent, solid scholars, and full of enthusiasm for learning—enthusiasm which they communicated to their pupils. In some respects indeed they resembled the rugged, earnest, scholarly Irishmen of old times, who travelled through Europe to spread religion and learning, as described at pp. 54, 55, farther on. But the famine of 1847 broke up those schools, and in a very few years they nearly all disappeared.

But our business here is mainly with the early monastic schools, which became so celebrated all over Europe. Before going farther it is well to remark that these schools also continued, and increased and multiplied as time went on. They held their ground successfully—as the lay schools did—during the evil days of later ages, when determined attempts were made, under the penal laws, to suppress them; and at the present day they are working all over the country quite as vigorously as in days of yore.

To notice all the monastic schools of old that attained eminence would demand more space than can be afforded here. So we must content ourselves with mentioning the following, all of which were very illustrious in their time:—Bangor (Co. Down), Lismore

13

(Co. Waterford), Clonmacnoise, Armagh, Kildare, Clonard (Meath),[Pg 43] Clonfert (Galway), Durrow (King's Co.), Monasterboice (near Drogheda), Rosscarbery (Co. Cork), and Derry. Besides these, at least twenty-five others, all eminent, are specially mentioned in our old books. Most of these colleges were working, not in succession, but all at the same time, from the sixth century downwards. When we bear in mind that there were also, during the whole period, the lay schools, which, though smaller, were far more numerous— scattered all over the country—we shall have some idea of the universal love of learning that existed in Ireland in those days, and of the general spread of education. No other nation in Europe could boast of so many schools and colleges in proportion to size and population.

Many of the monastic colleges had very large numbers of students. In Clonard there were 3,000, all residing in and around the college; and Bangor founded by St. Comgall, and Clonfert founded by St. Brendan the Navigator, had each as many. And there were various smaller numbers—2,000, 1,500, 1,000, 500—down to fifty.

The students were of all classes—rich and poor—from the sons of kings and chiefs down to the sons of farmers, tradesmen, and labourers; young laymen for general education, as well as[Pg 44] ecclesiastical students for the priesthood. All those who had the means paid their way in everything. But there were some who were so poor that they could pay little or nothing: and these 'poor scholars' (as they afterwards came to be called) received teaching, books, and often food, all free. But most of even the poorest did their best to pay something; and in this respect it is interesting to compare the usages of those long past times with some features of the college life of our own days. In some of the present American universities there is an excellent custom which enables very poor students to support themselves and pay their college fees. They wait on their richer comrades, bring up the dishes, etc., from the kitchen for meals, and lay the tables: and when the meal is over, they remove everything, wash up dishes and plates, and put them all by in their proper places. In fact, they perform most of the work expected from ordinary servants. For this they receive food and some small payment, which renders them independent of charity.

And the pleasing feature of this arrangement is, that it is not attended with any sense of humiliation or loss of self-respect. During study and lecture hours these same young men, having[Pg 45] put by aprons and napkins, and donned their ordinary dress, are received and treated on terms of perfect equality by those they have served, who take on no airs, and do not pose as superiors, but mix with them in free and kindly intercourse as fellow-students and comrades.

All this was anticipated in Ireland more than a thousand years ago; for a similar custom existed in some of the old Irish colleges. The very poor students often lived with some of their richer brethren, and acted as their servants, for which they received food and other kinds of payment. Many of these youths who served in this humble capacity subsequently became great and learned men, as indeed we might expect, for boys of this stamp are made of the best stuff; and some of them are now famed in our records as eminent fathers of the ancient Irish Church.

The greatest number of the students lived in houses built by themselves, or by hired workmen—some, mere huts, each for a single person; some, large houses, for several: and all around the central college buildings there were whole streets of these houses, often forming a good-sized town.

Where there were large numbers great care was taken that there should be no confusion or disorder. The whole school was commonly divided into[Pg 46] sections, over each of which was placed a leader or master, whose orders should be obeyed: and over the whole college there was one head-master or principal, usually called a *Fer-leginn*, i.e., 'Man of learning': while the abbot presided over all—monastery and college. The Fer-leginn was always some distinguished man—of course a great scholar. He was generally a monk, but sometimes a layman; for those good monks selected the best man they could find, whether priest or layman.

I suppose those who are accustomed to the grand universities and colleges of the present day, with their palatial buildings, would feel inclined to laugh at the simple, rough-and-ready methods and appliances of the old Irish colleges. There were no comfortable study rooms, well furnished with desks, seats, and rostrums: no spacious lecture halls. The

14

greater part of the work, indeed, was carried on in the open air when the weather at all permitted. At study time the students went just where they pleased, and accommodated themselves as best they could. All round the college you would see every flowery bank, every scented hedgerow, every green glade and sunny hillock occupied with students, sitting or lying down, or pacing thoughtfully, each with[Pg 47] his precious manuscript book open before him, all poring over the lesson assigned for next lecture, silent, attentive, and earnest.[3]

Then the little handbell tinkled for some particular lecture, and the special students for this hurried to their places, and seated themselves as best they could—on chair, stool, form, stone, or bank, and opened their books. These same books, too, were a motley collection—some large, some small, some fresh from the scribe, some tattered and brown with age: but all most carefully covered and preserved; for they were very expensive. You now buy a good school copy of some classical author for, say, half-a-crown: at that time it would probably cost what was equivalent to £2 of our present money.

Then the master went over the text, translating and explaining it, and whenever he thought it necessary questioned his pupils, to draw them out. After this he had to stand the cross-fire of the students' questions, who asked him to explain all sorts of difficulties: for this was one of the college regulations. There were no grammars,[Pg 48] no dictionaries, no simple introductory lesson books, such as we have now. The students had to go straight at the Latin or Greek text, and where they failed to make sense, the master stepped in with his help. And in this rugged and difficult fashion they mastered the language.

Yet it was in rude institutions of this kind that were educated those men whose names became renowned all over Europe, and who—for the period when they lived—are now honoured as among the greatest scholars and missionaries that the world ever saw.

The great Irish colleges were, in fact, universities in the full sense of the word, that is to say, schools which taught the whole circle of knowledge: they were, indeed, in a great measure the models on which our present universities were formed. The Latin and Greek languages and literatures were studied and taught with success. In science the Irish scholars were famous for their knowledge of Geometry, Arithmetic, Astronomy, Music, Geography, and so forth. And they were equally eminent in sacred learning—Theology, Divinity, and the Holy Scriptures.

The schools proved their mettle by the scholars they educated and sent forth: scholars[Pg 49] who astonished all Europe in their day. Sedulius of the fifth century (whose name is still represented by the family name Shiel), an eminent divine, orator, and poet, travelled into France, Italy, Greece, and Asia, and composed some beautiful Latin hymns, which are still used in the services of the Church. 'Fergil the Geometer' went in 745 from his monastery of Aghaboe in Queen's County to France, where he became famous for his deep scientific learning, and where he taught publicly—and probably for the first time—that the earth is round, having people living on the other side. John Scotus Erigena ('John the Irish-born Scot') of the ninth century taught in Paris; he was the greatest Greek scholar of his time, and was equally eminent in Theology. St. Columbanus of Bobbio (in Italy), a Leinsterman, a pupil of the college of Bangor, proved himself, while in France and Italy, a master of many kinds of learning, and was one of the greatest, most fearless, and most successful of the Irish missionaries on the Continent.

These men, and scores of others that we cannot find space for here, spread the fame of their native country everywhere. It was no wonder that the people of Great Britain and the Continent, when they met such scholars, all from Ireland,[Pg 50] came to the conclusion that the schools which educated them were the best to be found anywhere. Accordingly, students came from all parts of the known world, to place themselves under the masters of these schools. From Germany, France, Italy, Egypt, came priests and laymen, princes, chiefs, and peasant students—all eagerly seeking to drink from the fountain of Irish learning. And let us bear in mind that in those days it was a far more difficult, dangerous, and tedious undertaking to travel to Ireland from the interior of the European Continent, than it is now to go to Australia or China. But even in much greater numbers than these came students from Great Britain. An English writer of that period, who was jealous of the Irish schools and in very bad humour with his countrymen for coming to them, is nevertheless forced to

15

admit that Englishmen came to Ireland "in fleetloads." In our Histories of Ireland we have read of the real Irish welcome they received—as recorded by the Venerable Bede and by others—and how the Irish, not only taught them, but gave them books and food for nothing at all! It was quite a common thing that young Englishmen, after they had learned all that their own schools were able to teach them, came to Ireland to finish their education.

[Pg 51]The more the students crowded to the Irish schools, whether from Ireland itself or from abroad, the more eagerly did the masters strive to meet the demand, by studying more and more deeply the various branches of learning, so as to equal or excel the scholars of other countries. Then Ireland became the most learned country in Europe, so that it came at last to be known everywhere as 'The Island of Saints and Scholars.'

CHAPTER VII.
HOW IRISH MISSIONARIES AND SCHOLARS SPREAD RELIGION AND LEARNING IN FOREIGN COUNTRIES.

Towards the end of the sixth century the great body of the Irish were Christians, so that the holy men of Ireland were able to turn their attention to the conversion of other people. Then arose an extraordinary zeal for spreading religion and learning in foreign lands; and hundreds of devoted and determined missionaries left our shores. There was ample field for their noble ambition. For these were the Dark Ages, when the civilisation and learning bequeathed by old Greece and Rome had been almost wiped out of existence by the[Pg 52] barbarous northern hordes who overran Europe; and Christianity had not yet time to spread its softening influence among them. Through the greater part of England and Scotland, and over vast regions of the Continent, the teeming populations were fierce and ignorant, and sunk in gross superstition and idolatry, or with little or no religion at all.

To begin with the Irish missionary work in Great Britain. The people of Northern and Western Scotland, who were solidly pagan till the sixth century, were converted by St. Columkille and his monks from Iona, who were all Irishmen; for Iona was an Irish monastic colony founded by St. Columkille, a native of Tirconnell, now Donegal.

In the seven kingdoms of England—the Heptarchy—the Anglo-Saxons were the ruling race, rude and stubborn, and greatly attached to their gloomy northern pagan gods. We know that the kingdom of Kent was converted by the Roman missionary St. Augustine; but Christianity made little headway outside this till St. Aidan began his labours among the Northumbrian Saxons. Aidan was an Irishman who entered the monastery of Iona, from which he was sent to preach to the Northumbrians on the invitation of[Pg 53] their good king, Oswald. He founded the monastery of Lindisfarne, which afterwards became so illustrious. He was its first abbot; and for thirty years it was governed by him and by two other Irish abbots, Finan and Colman, in succession. He and his companions were wonderfully successful, so that the people of the large kingdom of Northumbria became Christians. Not only in Northumberland but all over England we find at the present day evidences of the active labours of the Irish missionaries in Great Britain.

Whole crowds of ardent and learned Irishmen travelled on the Continent in the sixth, seventh, and succeeding centuries, spreading Christianity and secular knowledge everywhere among the people. On this point we have the decisive testimony of an eminent French writer of the ninth century, Eric of Auxerre, who himself witnessed what he records. In a letter written by him to Charles the Bald, king of France, he says:—"What shall I say of Ireland, who, despising the dangers of the deep, is migrating with almost her whole train of philosophers to our coasts?" And other foreign evidences of a like kind might be brought forward.

These men, on their first appearance on the Continent, caused much surprise, they were so[Pg 54] startlingly different from those preachers the people had been accustomed to. They travelled on foot towards their destination in small companies, generally of thirteen. They wore a coarse outer woollen garment, in colour as it came from the fleece, and under this a white tunic of finer stuff. The long hair behind flowed down on the back: and the eyelids were painted or stained black. Each had a long stout walking-stick: and slung from the shoulder a leathern bottle for water, and a wallet containing his greatest treasure—a book or two and some relics. They spoke a strange language among themselves, used Latin to those who understood it, and made use of an interpreter when preaching, until they had learned the language of the place.

Few people have any idea of the trials and dangers they encountered. Most of them were persons in good position, who might have lived in plenty and comfort at home. They knew well, when setting out, that they were leaving country and friends probably for ever; for of those that went, very few returned. Once on the Continent, they had to make their way, poor and friendless, through people whose language they did not understand, and who were in many places ten times more rude and dangerous in those ages[Pg 55] than the inhabitants of these islands: and we know as a matter of history, that many were killed on the way. But these stout-hearted pilgrims were prepared for all this, and looking only to the service of their Master, never flinched. They were confident, cheerful, and self-helpful, faced privation with indifference, caring nothing for luxuries; and when other provisions failed them, they gathered wild fruit, trapped animals, and fished, with great dexterity and with any sort of next-to-hand rude appliances. They were somewhat rough in outward appearance: but beneath all that they had solid sense and much learning. Their simple ways, their unmistakable piety, and their intense earnestness in the cause of religion caught the people everywhere, so that they made converts in crowds.

A great French writer, Montalembert, speaks of the Irish of those days as having a "Passion for pilgrimage and preaching," and as feeling "under a stern necessity of spreading themselves abroad to combat paganism, and carry knowledge and faith afar." They were to be found everywhere through Europe, even as far as Iceland and the Faroe and Shetland Islands. Europe was too small for their missionary enterprise. Many were to be found in Egypt; and as early as the seventh[Pg 56] century, three learned Irish monks found their way to Carthage, where they laboured for a long time and with great success.

Wherever they went they made pilgrimages to holy places—places sanctified by memories of early saints—and whenever they found it practicable they were sure to make their way to Rome, to visit the shrines of the apostles, and obtain the blessing of the Pope.

The Irish "passion for pilgrimage and preaching" never died out: it is a characteristic of the race. This great missionary emigration to foreign lands has continued in a measure down to our own day: for it may be safely asserted that no other missionaries are playing so general and successful a part in the conversion of the pagan people all over the world, and in keeping alight the lamp of religion among Christians, as those of Ireland.

Irishmen were equally active in spreading secular knowledge. Indeed the two functions were generally combined; for it was quite common to find a man a successful missionary, while at the same time acting as professor in a college, or as head of some great seminary for general education. Irish professors and teachers were in those times held in such estimation that[Pg 57] they were employed in most of the schools and colleges of Great Britain, France, Germany, and Italy. The revival of learning on the Continent was indeed due in no small degree to those Irish missionaries. It was enough that the candidate for an appointment came from Ireland: he needed no other recommendation.

When learning had declined in England in the ninth and tenth centuries, owing to the devastations of the Danes, it was chiefly by Irish teachers it was kept alive and restored. In Glastonbury especially, they taught with great success. We are told by English writers that "they were skilled in every department of learning sacred and profane"; and that under them were educated many young English nobles, sent to Glastonbury with that object. Among these students the most distinguished was St. Dunstan, who, according to all his biographers, received his education, both Scriptural and secular, from Irish masters there.

As for the numerous Continental schools and colleges in which Irishmen figured either as principals or professors, it would be impossible, with our limited space, to notice them here. A few have been glanced at in the last chapter; and I will finish this short narrative by relating[Pg 58] the odd manner in which two distinguished Irishmen, brothers, named Clement and Albinus,[4] began their career on the Continent.

One of the historians of the reign of Charlemagne, who wrote in the ninth century, has left us the following account of these two scholars:—When the illustrious Charles began to reign alone in the western parts of the world, and literature was almost forgotten, it happened that two Scots from Ireland came over with some British merchants to the shores of France, men incomparably skilled in human learning and in the Holy Scriptures. Observing how the merchants exhibited and drew attention to their wares, they acted in a similar fashion to force themselves into notice like the others. They went through the market-place among the crowds, and cried out to them:—"If there be any who want wisdom (*i.e.*, learning), let them come to us, for we have it to sell." This they repeated as they went from place to place, so that the people wondered very much; and some thought them to be nothing more than persons half crazed.

Strange rumours regarding them went round,[Pg 59] and at length came to the ears of King Charles; on which he sent for the brothers, and had them brought to his presence. He questioned them closely, using the Latin language, and asked them whether it was really the case that they had learning; and they replied—in the same language—that they had, and were ready, in the name of God, to communicate it to those who sought it with worthy intentions. Then the king asked what payment they would expect, and they replied:—"We require proper houses and accommodation, pupils with ingenious minds and really anxious to learn; and, as we are in a foreign country where we cannot conveniently work for our bread, we shall require food and raiment: we want nothing more."

Now at this very time King Charles was using his best efforts to restore learning, by opening schools throughout his dominions, but found it hard to procure a sufficient supply of qualified teachers. And as he perceived that these brothers were evidently men of real learning, and of a superior cast in every way, he joyfully accepted their proposals. Having kept them for some time on a visit in his palace, he finally opened a great school in some part of France—probably Paris—for the education of boys of all[Pg 60] ranks of society, not only for the sons of the highest nobles, but also for those of the middle and low classes, at the head of which he placed Clement. He also directed that all the scholars should be provided with food and suitable habitations: it was in fact a great free boarding-school, founded and maintained at the expense of the king. As for Albinus, he sent him to Italy, with directions that he should be placed at the head of the important school of the monastery of St. Augustine at Pavia. And these schools are now remembered in history as two great and successful centres of learning belonging to those ages.

CHAPTER VIII.
HOW THE ANCIENT IRISH WROTE DOWN ALL THEIR LITERATURE, AND HOW BOOKS INCREASED AND MULTIPLIED.

Printing was not invented till the fifteenth century, and before that time all books had of course to be written by hand.

According to our native records the art of writing was known to the pagan Irish, and the[Pg 61] druids had books on law and other subjects, long before the time of St. Patrick. Besides these home evidences, which are so numerous and strong as hardly to admit of dispute, we have the testimony of a learned foreigner, which is quite decisive on the point. A Christian philosopher of the fourth century of our era, named Ethicus of Istria, travelled over the three continents, and has left a description of his wanderings, in what he calls a 'Cosmography' of the World. He visited Ireland more than a hundred years before the arrival of St. Patrick; and he states that he found there many books, and that he remained for some time in the country examining them. So far then as Ethicus records the existence of Irish books in the fourth century, he merely corroborates our own native accounts.

The pagan Irish books were, of course, written in the Irish language; but as to the nature or shapes of the letters, or the form of the writing, or how it reached Ireland, on these points we have no information, for none of the old books remain. The letters used in these books could hardly have been what are known as Ogham characters, for these are too cumbrous for long passages.

Ogham was a species of writing, the letters of which were formed by combinations of short lines[Pg 62] and points, on and at both sides of a middle or stem line. Nearly all the

Oghams hitherto found are sepulchral inscriptions. Great numbers of monumental stones are preserved with Ogham inscriptions cut on them, of which most have been deciphered, either partially or completely. They are in a very antique form of the Irish language; and while many were engraved in far distant pagan ages, others belong to Christian times.

But whatever characters the Irish may have used in times of paganism, they learned the Roman letters from the early Roman missionaries, and adopted them in writing their own language during and after the time of St. Patrick: which are still retained in modern Irish. These same letters, moreover, were brought to Great Britain by the early Irish missionaries already spoken of (p. 52), from whom the Anglo-Saxons learned them; so that England received her first knowledge of the letters of the alphabet—as she received most of her Christianity—from Ireland. Formerly it was the fashion to call those letters Anglo-Saxon: but now people know better. Our present printed characters—the very characters now under the reader's eye—were ultimately developed from those old Irish-Roman letters.

After the time of St. Patrick, as everything[Pg 63] seems to have been written down that was considered worth preserving, Manuscripts accumulated in the course of time, which were kept in monasteries and in the houses of professors of learning: many also in the libraries of private persons. The most general material used for writing on was vellum or parchment, made from the skins of sheep, goats, or calves. To copy a book was justly considered a very meritorious work, and in the highest degree so if it was a part of the Holy Scriptures, or of any other book on sacred or devotional subjects. Scribes or copyists were therefore much honoured. The handwriting of these old documents is remarkable for its beauty, its plainness, and its perfect uniformity; each scribe, however, having his own characteristic form and style.

Sometimes the scribes wrote down what had never been written before, that is, matters composed at the time, or preserved in memory; but more commonly they copied from other volumes. If an old book began to be worn, ragged, or dim with age, so as to be hard to make out and read, some scribe was sure to copy it, so as to have a new book easy to read and well bound up. Most of the books written out in this manner related to Ireland, as will be described presently; and[Pg 64] the language of these was almost always Irish; except in copies of the Roman classics or of the Scriptures, where Latin was used.

Books abounded in Ireland when the Danes first made their appearance, about the beginning of the ninth century; so that the old Irish writers often speak with pride of "the hosts of the books of Erin." But with the first Danish arrivals began the woeful destruction of manuscripts, the records of ancient learning. The animosity of the barbarians was specially directed against books, monasteries, and monuments of religion: and all the manuscripts they could lay hold on they either burned or "drowned"—*i.e.*, flung them into the nearest lake or river. Next came the Anglo-Norman Invasion, which was quite as destructive of native books, learning, and art as the Danish inroads, or more so; and most of the old volumes that survived were scattered and lost.

Notwithstanding all this havoc and wreck, we have still preserved a large number of old Irish books. The ornamented and illuminated copies of the Scriptures are described in the chapter on Art. We have also many volumes of Miscellaneous Literature in which are written compositions of all kinds, both prose and poetry, copied from older books, and written in, one after another, till the[Pg 65] volume was filled. Of all these old books of mixed compositions, the largest that remains to us is the Book of Leinster, which is kept in Trinity College, Dublin. It is an immense volume, all in the Irish language, written more than 750 years ago; and many of the pages are now almost black with age and very hard to make out. It contains a great number of pieces, some in prose and some in verse, and nearly all of them about Ireland:—histories, accounts of battles and sieges, lives and adventures of great men, with many tales and stories of things that happened in this country in far distant ages.

The Book of the Dun Cow is preserved in the Royal Irish Academy in Dublin. It is fifty years older than the Book of Leinster, but not so large; and it contains also a great number of tales, adventures, and histories, all relating to Ireland, and all in the Irish language.

Two other great Irish books kept in Dublin are the Yellow Book of Lecan [Leckan] and the Book of Ballymote. These contain much the same kind of matter as the Book of Leinster—with pieces mostly different however—but they are not nearly so old. The

Speckled Book, which is also in Dublin, is nearly as large as the Book of Leinster, but not so old. It is mostly on[Pg 66] religious matters, and contains a great number of Lives of saints, hymns, sermons, portions of the Scriptures, and other such pieces. All these books are written with the greatest care, and in most beautiful penmanship.

The five old books described above have been lately printed, in such a way that the print resembles exactly the writing of the old books themselves. The printed volumes are now to be found in libraries in several parts of Ireland, as well as in England and on the Continent; so that those desirous of studying them need not come to Dublin, as people had to do formerly. Another grand old book preserved in Dublin is the Book of Lecan. Besides these there are vast numbers of Irish manuscript books in Dublin and elsewhere, both vellum and paper, having no special names, all containing important and interesting pieces. There are also numerous books of law, of medicine, of science, genealogies, Lives of saints, sermons, and so forth, which on account of limited space cannot be described here.

Many people are now eagerly studying these books; and men often come to Ireland from France, Germany, Italy, Norway, Sweden, Russia, and other countries, in order to learn the Irish language so as to be able to read them. But this requires[Pg 67] much study, even from those who know the Irish of the present day; for the language of these books is old and difficult.

CHAPTER IX.
HOW THE IRISH SCHOLARS COMPILED THEIR ANNALS.

Among the various classes of persons who devoted themselves to Literature in ancient Ireland, there were special Annalists, who made it their business to record, with the utmost accuracy, all remarkable events simply and briefly, year by year. The extreme care they took that their statements should be truthful is shown by the manner in which they compiled their books. As a general rule they admitted nothing into their records except either what occurred during their lifetime, and which may be said to have come under their own personal knowledge, or what they found recorded in the compilations of previous annalists, who had themselves followed the same plan. These men took nothing on hearsay: and in this manner successive annalists carried on a continued chronicle from age to age.

[Pg 68]We have still preserved to us many books of native Annals. They deal with the affairs of Ireland—generally but not exclusively. Many of them record events occurring in other parts of the world; and it was a common practice to begin the work with a brief general history, after which the annalist takes up the affairs of Ireland.

There are many tests which prove the remarkable accuracy of the Irish Annals. For instance, their records of such occurrences as eclipses, comets, tides, and so forth, are invariably found to be correct. Indeed they could not be otherwise, for the good reason that the faithful chronicler noted down the events, each at the very time of its occurrence. If he waited for some future time, or noted down some event that had occurred years before, taking hearsay evidence, or calculating the time backwards as best he could, the chances were that there would be an error in the date.

A remarkable example occurs in the record of an eclipse of the sun of A.D. 664. At the present day astronomers can calculate to a minute the time of an eclipse occurring in that or any other year. But it was otherwise twelve centuries ago. Then the rules of calculation[Pg 69] were not quite correct, so that a person calculating backwards was pretty sure to be in error as to the exact time. The great English historian and scholar, the Venerable Bede, who wrote fifty or sixty years after the above-mentioned eclipse, was aware of the year (664), but had to calculate the day and the hour. The rule then in vogue led him astray, and accordingly his record of the date—the 3rd May—is two days wrong. In the Annals of Ulster the correct date—1st May, 664—is given, and even the very hour. This shows quite clearly that the event had been recorded by some Irish chronicler, who actually saw it and noted it down on the spot. We find numbers of records of this kind in our Annals, which, according to the accurate tests we are now able to apply, are all found to be correct.

Another remarkable instance of a similar kind deserves to be mentioned here. We have an old Irish book called "The War of the Irish with the Danes," written early in the eleventh century, soon after the battle of Clontarf, in which that great battle is very fully described. In the course of his narrative the writer makes these very specific statements:—that the battle was fought on Good Friday, the 23rd April, 1014; that it commenced at sunrise *when the tide was*[Pg 70] *full in*, and that it lasted the whole day till the tide was again at flood about the same hour in the evening, when the foreigners were routed. Moreover, the old historian puts in the time of high water, morning and afternoon, merely to explain why there was such terrible slaughter of the Danes in the evening; for on account of the full tide they were not able to reach their ships, which lay some distance out in the bay, whereas if it had been low water they might have waded out to them. Beyond that he was not in the least concerned about the time of high tide.

The tide comes in at any particular point of the coast about every 12 hours 25 minutes, and accordingly the hour changes from day to day, so that there might be a high tide at any hour of the twenty-four: but astronomers can now calculate the exact time of high tide for any day of the month at a particular place in any year, no matter how far back. Now, the question is, was the tide really at its height on the Clontarf shore at sunrise on that fatal morning?

Forty years ago, the Rev. Dr. Todd, who was then engaged in translating the old book mentioned above, in order to test the chronicler's accuracy, put this question to the Rev. Dr. Haughton, a great science scholar, of Trinity[Pg 71] College, Dublin:—At what time was there high tide in Dublin Bay on the 23rd April, 1014? After a laborious calculation, Dr. Haughton found that the tide was at its height that morning at half-past five o'clock, just as the sun was coming over the horizon, and that the evening tide was in at fifty-five minutes past five: a striking confirmation of the truth of this part of the narrative. It shows, too, that the account was written by or taken down from an eye-witness of the battle. Dr. Haughton's calculation—every figure—may now be seen in Dr. Todd's published book.

Little did the old annalist think, when penning his simple record, that after lying by unnoticed and forgotten on some obscure bookshelf for eight centuries, it was destined to be at last brought out under the broad light of science, and its accuracy fully tested and established.

There are several other ways of testing the truth of our annals. One is by comparing them with the testimony of foreign writers of good standing. Events occurring in Ireland in those early ages are not often mentioned by British or Continental writers. Indeed they knew very little about Ireland, which was, in those times, especially as regards the Continent, a very remote[Pg 72] place. But whenever they do notice Irish affairs, it may be said that they are always in agreement with the native records.

In our Irish books we find accounts of events or customs, which some people—not knowing better—would be inclined to pronounce fabulous, but which we find recorded as sober history by certain great English and Continental historians. The colonisation of Scotland from Ireland, for instance, which was formerly doubted by many, is fully confirmed by the Venerable Bede. And to take another instance from the battle of Clontarf:—All the Irish chronicles state that a general rout of the Danes took place in the evening, and that there was an awful slaughter of them, for they were cut off from their fortress by the river Liffey, and from their ships by the high tide; while the infuriated Irish assailed them, front, flank, and rear. Now in the description of the battle by a Danish writer—the best possible authority in the case, as he had good reason to know what happened—there is a full confirmation of this. His record is simple and plain:—"Then flight broke out throughout all the Danish host."

The more the ancient historical records of Ireland are examined and tested, the more their truthfulness is made manifest. Their uniform[Pg 73] agreement among themselves, and their accuracy, as tried by various tests, have drawn forth the acknowledgments of the greatest Irish scholars and archæologists that ever lived.

The existing books of Irish Annals will be found described in our Histories of Ireland, and more fully in the two Social Histories of Ancient Ireland. Most of them have been published with translations. Here we must content ourselves with mentioning one, the

21

Annals of the Four Masters, the most important of all. These were compiled in the Franciscan monastery of Donegal, by three of the O'Clerys, and by Ferfesa O'Mulconry, who are now commonly known as the 'Four Masters.' They began in 1632, and completed the work in 1636. The Annals of the Four Masters was translated with most elaborate and learned annotations by Dr. John O'Donovan; and it was published—Irish text, translation, and notes—in seven large volumes.

The *Dinnsenchus* [Din-shannahus] is a treatise giving the history and derivations of the names of remarkable hills, caves, raths, lakes, rivers, fords, and so forth. Another corresponding treatise for the names of noted Irish historical persons is called the *Cóir Anmann*, meaning 'fitness of names.' Both have been translated and published.

[Pg 74]
CHAPTER X.
HOW THE IRISH DERIVED AMUSEMENT AND INSTRUCTION FROM HISTORICAL AND ROMANTIC TALES.

From the earliest date, the Irish people, like those of other countries, had Stories, which, before the introduction of the art of writing, were transmitted orally, and modified, improved, and enlarged as time went on, by successive *shanachies*, or 'storytellers.' They began to be written down when writing became general: and it has been shown by scholars that the main tales assumed their present forms in the seventh, eighth, and ninth centuries; while the originals from which they sprang were much older. Once they began to be written down, a great body of romantic and historical written literature rapidly accumulated, consisting chiefly of prose tales. They are contained in our old manuscripts, from the Book of the Dun Cow downwards.

The chief use of popular tales all the world over was—and is—to amuse. The storyteller recited the narrative for his audience, who listened because it gave them pleasure. But in Ireland[Pg 75] the native stories were turned to another important use:—they were made to help in educating the people in the manner explained farther on. Besides this use a large part of the History of Ireland is derived from the historic tales; and it is proper to remark here that the early histories of England, France, Germany, and other countries, as we find them now presented to us by the best and most reliable modern authors, are largely derived from similar sources.

The construction and arrangement of the tales were carefully studied by the Irish literary men of the olden time, and not more than their importance deserved. They were arranged in seventeen classes or groups, and in each group there were a number of individual stories. This grouping was a great help to the storyteller, who had to store up in his memory a large number of tales: for by having them in this manner, sorted as it were in parcels, he was enabled to call them up all the more readily—to put his hand on them, so to say—when he wanted them. 'Voyages,' for instance, formed one group, which included "The Voyage of Maeldune," "The Voyage of St. Brendan," "The Voyage of the Sons of O'Corra," and many others. Another was 'Tragedies,' under which came "The Fate of the Children of Lir," "The[Pg 76] Fate of the Sons of Usna," etc., etc. There were 'Military Expeditions,' 'Courtships,' 'Cattle-raids,' 'Sieges,' and so on, to the number of seventeen, each group with its own parcel of stories.

We have in our old books stories belonging to every one of these classes. The whole number now existing in manuscripts is close on 600: of which about 150 have been published and translated. But outside these, great numbers have been lost: destroyed during the Danish and Anglo-Norman wars.

Most of the Irish tales fall under four main cycles or periods of history and legend, which, in all the Irish poetical and romantic literature, were kept quite distinct.

First:—The Mythological Period, the stories of which are concerned with the mythical colonies preceding the Milesians, especially the Dedannans. The heroes of the tales belonging to this cycle, who are assigned to periods long before the Christian era, are gods, namely, the gods of the pagan Irish.

Second.—The Period of Concobar mac Nessa and his Red Branch Knights, who flourished in the first century. These Red Branch Knights were a sort of heroic militia, belonging to Ulster, mighty men all, who came every year to the palace of Emain to be trained in military science and feats[Pg 77] of arms, residing for the time in a separate palace called Creeveroe or the Red Branch. Their greatest commander was Cuculainn, a demigod, the mightiest of all the Irish heroes of antiquity, whose residence was Dundalgan, now called the Fort of Castletown, near Dundalk. Others of these great heroes were Conall Kernagh, Laery the Victorious, Keltar of the Battles, Fergus mac Roy, and the three Sons of Usna— Naisi, Ainnle, and Ardan. They were in the service of Concobar or Conor mac Nessa, king of Ulster, who feasted the leading heroes every day in his own palace.

Third.—The Period of the Fena of Erin, belonging to a time two centuries later than the stories of the Red Branch. The Fena of Erin, who flourished in the time of King Cormac mac Art, in the third century, were a body of militia kept for the defence of the throne, very like the Red Branch Knights. Their most celebrated leader was King Cormac's son-in-law, Finn, the son of Cumal—or Finn mac Coole, as he is commonly called—who of all the ancient heroes of Ireland is at the present day best remembered in tradition. We have in our old manuscripts many beautiful stories of these Fena, like those of the Red Branch Knights.

[Pg 78]*Fourth.*—Stories founded on events that happened after the dispersal of the Fena (in the end of the third century). Many fine stories—nearly all of them more or less historical—belong to this Period.

The stories of the Red Branch Knights form the finest part of our ancient Romantic Literature. The most celebrated of all these is the Táin-bo-Quelně, the epic or main heroic story of Ireland. It relates how Maive, queen of Connaught, who resided in her palace of Croghan, set out with her army for Ulster on a plundering expedition, attended by all the great heroes of Connaught. The invading army entered that part of Ulster called Quelna or Cooley, the territory of the hero Cuculainn, the north part of the present county Louth, including the Carlingford peninsula. At this time the Ulstermen were under a spell of feebleness, all but Cuculainn, who had to defend single-handed the several fords and passes, in a series of single combats, against Maive's best champions. She succeeded in this first raid, notwithstanding Cuculainn's heroic defence, and brought away a great brown bull—which was the chief motive of the expedition—with flocks and herds beyond number. At length, the Ulstermen, having been freed from the spell, pursued the[Pg 79] raiders, and attacked and routed the Connaught army. The battles, single combats, and other incidents of this war, form the subject of the Táin, which consists of one main story, with about thirty shorter tales grouped round it.

Of the Cycle of Finn and the Fena of Erin we have a vast collection of stories. In these we read about Finn himself and his mighty exploits; about Ossian his son, the renowned hero-poet; about Oscar the brave and gentle, the son of Ossian; about Dermot O'Dyna, brave, honourable, generous, and self-denying, perhaps the finest hero of any literature; and many others. The Tales of the Fena, though not so old as those of the Red Branch Knights, are still of great antiquity.

Some of the Irish tales are historical, *i.e.*, founded on historical events—history embellished with some fiction; while others are altogether fictitious—creations of the imagination, but always woven round historical personages. From this great body of stories it would be easy to select a large number, powerful in conception and execution, very beautiful, high and dignified in tone and feeling, many of them worthy to rank with the best literature of their kind in any language. The stories of the Sons of Usna,[5] the Children[Pg 80] of Lir,[6] the Fingal Ronain, the Voyage of Maeldune,[6] The Voyage of the Sons of O'Corra,[6] Da Derga's Hostel, The Pursuit of Dermot and Grania,[6] the Boroma, and the Fairy Palace of the Quicken Trees[6]—all of which have been published with translations— are only a few instances in point. And it would be easy to name many others if our space permitted.

On the score of morality and purity the Irish tales can compare favourably with the corresponding literature of other countries; and they are much freer from objectionable matter than the works of many of those early English and Continental authors which are now regarded as classics. Of one large collection of Irish tales, the great Irish scholar Dr.

23

Whitley Stokes, a Dublin man, says:—"The tales are generally told with sobriety and directness: they evince genuine feeling for natural beauty, a passion for music, a moral purity, singular in a mediæval collection of stories, a noble love of manliness and honour." On the Irish Tales in general Dr. Kuno Meyer, a German, one of the greatest living Celtic scholars, justly remarks:—"The literature of no nation is free from occasional grossness; and considering the great antiquity of Irish literature, and the[Pg 81] primitive life which it reflects, what will strike an impartial observer most is not its license or coarseness, but rather the purity, loftiness, and tenderness which pervade it."

The tales were brought into direct touch with the people, not by reading—for there were few books outside libraries, and few people were able to read them—but by Recitation: and the Irish of all classes, like the Greeks, were excessively fond of hearing tales and poetry recited. There were professional shanachies and poets whose duty it was to know by heart numerous old tales, poems, and historical pieces, and to recite them at festive gatherings for the entertainment of the chiefs and their guests: and every intelligent person was supposed to know a reasonable number of them by heart, so as to be always ready to take a part in amusing and instructing his company.

The tales of those times correspond with the novels and historical romances of our own day, and served a purpose somewhat similar. Indeed they served a much higher purpose than the generality of our novels; for in conjunction with poetry they were the chief agency in education—education in the best sense of the word—a real healthful informing exercise for the intellect.[Pg 82] They conveyed a knowledge of history and geography, and they inculcated truthfulness, manliness, help for the weak, and all that was noble and dignified in thought, word, and action. Along with this, the greater part of the history, tradition, biography, and topography of the country, as well as history and geography in general, was thrown into the form of verse and tales, so that the person who knew a large number of them was well educated, according to what was required in those times. Moreover, this education was universal; for, though few could read, the knowledge and recitation of poetry and stories reached the whole body of the people. This ancient institution of story-telling held its ground both in Ireland and Scotland down to a period within living memory.

CHAPTER XI.
HOW THE ANCIENT IRISH EXCELLED IN MUSIC.

From the very earliest ages Irish musicians were celebrated for their skill, not only in their own country but all over Europe. Our native literature, whether referring to pagan or Christian[Pg 83] times, is full of references to music and to skilful musicians, who are always spoken of in terms of the utmost respect.

Everywhere through the Records we find evidences that the ancient Irish, both high and low, were passionately fond of music. It was mixed up with their daily home-life, and formed part of their amusements, meetings, and celebrations of every kind. In the religious tales music is always one of the delights of heaven; and a chief function of the angels who attend on God is to chant music of ineffable sweetness to Him, which they generally do in the shape of beautiful white birds. A good example of the people's intense fondness for music is found in an old Irish religious poem, in which the hard lot of Adam and Eve for a whole year after their expulsion from Paradise is described, when they were—as the poem expresses it—"without proper food, fire, house, *music*, or raiment." Here music is put among the necessaries of life, so that it was a misery to be without it.

In the early ages of the Church many of the Irish ecclesiastics took delight in playing on the harp; and in order to indulge in this innocent and refining taste they were wont to bring with them, on their missionary journeys, a small[Pg 84] portable harp, with which they beguiled many a weary hour after their hard work.

In very early times Irish professors of music were as eagerly sought after on the Continent as those of literature and general learning, so that they were sometimes placed at the head of great music-schools. At a later time it was quite common among the Welsh bards to come over to Ireland to receive instruction from the Irish harpers. In the eleventh century one of the Welsh kings, Griffith ap Conan, brought over to Wales a number of skilled Irish musicians, who, in conference with the native Welsh bards, carried out some great improvements in Welsh music. Ireland was long the school for Scottish harpers also, who regularly came over, like those of Wales, to finish their musical education—a practice which continued down to about 150 years ago.

Giraldus Cambrensis, a Welshman, who visited Ireland in 1185, though very much prejudiced against the Irish, says that Irish harpers were incomparably more skilful than those of any other nation he had ever heard play. From that period, in spite of wars and troubles, music continued to be cultivated, and there was an unbroken succession of great professional harpers, till the end of the eighteenth century, when,[Pg 85] for want of encouragement in the miserable condition of the country under the penal laws, the race died out.

The Harp is mentioned in the earliest Irish literature: it is constantly mixed up with our oldest legends; and it was in use from the remotest pagan times. The old Irish harps were of a medium size, or rather small, the average height being about thirty inches: and some were not much more than half that height. They had strings of brass wire which were tuned by a key, not very different from the present tuning-key. Irish harpers always played with the fingers or with the finger-nails.

The Irish had a small stringed instrument called a Timpan, which had only a few strings. It had a body like a flat drum, to which at one side was attached a short neck: the strings were stretched across the flat face of the drum and along the neck: and were tuned and regulated by pins or keys and a bridge. It was played with a bow or with the finger-nail, or by both together, while the notes were regulated in pitch—or 'stopped' as musicians say—with the fingers of the left hand, like those of a fiddle or guitar. This little instrument was a great favourite, and is constantly mentioned in Irish literature.

[Pg 86]Harpers and timpanists were honoured in Ireland beyond all other musicians; and their rights and privileges were even laid down in the law. Kings had always harpers in their service, who resided in the palaces and were well paid for their services.

The harp and timpan were the chief instruments of the higher classes, many of whom played them as an accomplishment, as people now play the piano and guitar. But the bagpipe was the great favourite of the common people. The form in use was what we now call the Highland or Scotch pipes—slung from the shoulder: the bag inflated by the mouth. This form of pipes took its rise in Ireland: and it was brought to Scotland in early ages by those Irish colonists already spoken of (page 11). There is another and a better kind of bagpipes, now common in Ireland, resting on the lap when in use, and having the bag inflated by a bellows: but this is a late invention.

The old Irish had also Whistles and Flageolets, with holes for the fingers and blown by the mouth, much like those of the present day. Some flageolets were double, and some even triple, i.e., with two, or with three, pipes, sounded by a single mouthpiece, and having holes which were all stopped by the fingers. On many of the[Pg 87] great stone crosses are sculptured harp-players and pipe-players, from which we learn a great deal about the shapes and sizes of the several instruments.

The Irish had curved bronze Trumpets and Horns of various shapes and sizes, which, judging from the numbers found buried in clay and bogs, must have been in very general use. In the National Museum in Dublin is a collection of twenty-six ancient trumpets, varying in length from 8 feet down to 18 inches. The larger ones are of most admirable workmanship, formed by hammering; curved, jointed, ornamented, and riveted with extraordinary skill and perfection of finish.

Among the household of every king and chief there was a band of trumpeters—as there were harpers—who were assigned their proper places at feasts and meetings. Trumpets were used for various purposes:—in war; in hunting; for signals during meetings and banquets; as a mark of honour on the arrival of distinguished visitors; and such like. For war purposes, trumpeters had different calls for directing movements—for battle, for unyoking, for marching, for halting, for retiring to sleep, for going into council, and so forth.

[Pg 88]The ancient Irish were very fond of a *Craebh ciuil* [crave-cule], or 'musical branch,' a little branch on which were suspended a number of diminutive bells, which produced a sweet tinkling when shaken: a custom found also in early times on the Continent. The musical branch figures much in Irish romantic literature.

The music of ancient Ireland consisted wholly of short airs, each with two strains or parts—seldom more. But these, though simple in comparison with modern music, were constructed with such exquisite art that of a large proportion of them it may be truly said no modern composer can produce airs of a similar kind to equal them.

The Irish musicians had various '*Styles*,' three of which are very often mentioned in tales and other ancient Irish writings: of these, numerous specimens have come down to the present day. The style they called 'Mirth-music' (*Ganntree*) consisted of lively airs, which excited to cheerfulness, mirthfulness, and laughter. These are represented by our present dance tunes, such as jigs, reels, hornpipes, and other such spirited pieces, which are known so well in every part of Ireland. The 'Sorrow-music' (*Goltree*) was slow and sad, and was always sung on the occasion of a death. We have many airs belonging[Pg 89] to this style, which are now commonly called *Keens*, i.e., laments, or dirges. The 'Sleep-music' (*Suantree*) was intended to produce sleep; and the tunes belonging to this style were plaintive and soothing. Such airs are now known as lullabies, or nurse-tunes, or cradle-songs, of which numerous examples are preserved in collections of Irish music. They were usually sung to put children to sleep. Though there are many tunes belonging to these three classes, they form only a small part of the great body of Irish music.

Music—as already remarked—entered into many of the daily occupations of the people. There were special spinning-wheel songs, which the women sang, with words, in chorus or in dialogue, when employed in spinning. At milking-time the girls were in the habit of chanting a particular sort of air, in a low gentle voice. These Milking-songs were slow and plaintive, something like the nurse-tunes, and had the effect of soothing the cows and of making them submit more gently to be milked. This practice was common down to fifty or sixty years ago; and I well remember seeing cows grow restless when the song was interrupted, and become again quiet and placid when it was resumed. The same custom was common in the Highlands of Scotland.[Pg 90] While ploughmen were at their work they whistled a sweet, slow, and sad strain, which had as powerful an effect in soothing the horses at their hard labour as the milking-songs had on the cows: and these Plough-whistles also were quite usual till about half a century ago.

Special airs and songs were used during working time by smiths, by weavers, and by boatmen. There were, besides, hymn-tunes; and young people had simple airs for all sorts of games and sports. In most cases words suitable to the several occasions were sung with lullabies, laments, and occupation-tunes. Examples of all the preceding classes of melodies will be found in the collections of Irish airs by Bunting, Petrie, and Joyce.

The Irish had numerous war-marches, which the pipers played at the head of the clansmen when marching to battle, and which inspired them with courage and dash for the fight. This custom is still kept up by the Scotch; and many fine battle-tunes are printed in Irish and Scotch collections of national music.

The man who did most in modern times to draw attention to Irish music was Thomas Moore. He composed his exquisite songs to old Irish airs. They at once became popular, not only in the[Pg 91] British Islands, but on the Continent and in America; and Irish music was thenceforward studied and admired where it would have never been heard of but for Moore.

Of the entire body of Irish airs that are preserved, we know the authors of only a very small proportion; and these were composed within the last two hundred years. Most of the remaining airs have come down from old times, scattered fragments of exquisite beauty that remind us of the refined musical culture of our forefathers. No one now can tell who composed "The Coolin," "Savourneen Dheelish," "Shule Aroon," "Molly Asthore," "Eileen Aroon," "Garryowen," "The Boyne Water," "Patrick's Day," "Langolee," "The Blackbird," or "The Girl I left behind me"; and so of many other well-known and lovely airs.

The national music of Ireland and that of Scotland are very like each other, and many airs are common to both countries: but this is only what might be expected, as we know that the Irish and the Highland Scotch were originally one people, and kept up mutual intercourse down to recent times.

CHAPTER XII.
HOW THE ANCIENT IRISH EXCELLED IN ART.

The old Irish people became wonderfully skilful in some branches of Art; and many specimens of their handiwork still remain—preserved through the wreck of ages—which exceed in beauty of design and in perfection of execution all works of the kind done by the artists of other nations.

While Art was cultivated in several branches, the Irish attained more skill in Ornamental Penwork than in any other. They took special delight, and used their utmost efforts, in ornamenting religious and devotional books, especially the Gospels and other parts of the Holy Scripture; for they justly considered that to beautify the sacred writings was one way of honouring and glorifying God.

The special Irish style of pen ornamentation was developed by successive generations of artists, who brought it to marvellous perfection. Its most marked feature is interlaced work formed by bands and ribbons, which are curved and twisted and interwoven in the most intricate[Pg 93] way, something like basket-work infinitely varied in pattern. Here and there among the complicated designs may be seen strange half-formed faces of animals, and sometimes human faces, or full figures of men or of angels. But vegetable forms are very rare.

What most astonishes a person examining this work is the amazing variety and minuteness of the patterns, and the perfect smoothness and evenness of the curves, as if they had been traced by compasses or some other fine instruments; though they were all drawn by the unaided hand. The scribes usually made the capital letters very large, so as sometimes to fill almost an entire page; and on these they exerted their utmost skill. They painted the open spaces of the letters and ornaments in brilliant colours: and in this art—an art usually designated 'Illumination'—the old Irish scribes also excelled.

Several manuscript-books, ornamented in this manner, have been preserved, of which it will be sufficient to mention one here—The Book of Kells, now in Trinity College, Dublin, though there are several others almost equally beautiful. It is a copy of the Four Gospels in Latin, written on vellum in the seventh or eighth century. Miss Margaret Stokes, of Dublin, a skilled artist[Pg 94] and a great judge of such matters, who has carefully examined this book, thus speaks of it:—"No effort hitherto made to transcribe any one page of this book has the perfection of execution and rich harmony of colour which belongs to this wonderful book. It is no exaggeration to say that, as with the microscopic works of nature, the stronger the magnifying power brought to bear upon it, the more is this perfection seen. No single false interlacement or uneven curve in the spirals, no faint trace of a trembling hand or wandering thought can be detected. This is the very passion of labour and devotion, and thus did the Irish scribe work to glorify his book."

Professor Westwood, of Oxford—an English gentleman—who examined the best specimens of penwork all over Europe, speaks even more strongly. "The Book of Kells," he says, "is the most astonishing book of the Four Gospels which exists in the world. How men could have had eyes and tools to work out the designs, I am sure I, with all the skill and knowledge in such kind of work which I have been exercising for the last fifty years, cannot conceive. I know pretty well all the libraries in Europe where such books as this occur, but there is no such[Pg 95] book in any of them. There is nothing like it in all the books which were written for Charlemagne and his successors."

There was a book like this, long since lost, in St. Brigit's convent of Kildare, which was shown to the Welshman Giraldus Cambrensis more than seven hundred years ago, and which so astonished him that he has recorded a legend—to which he devotes a separate chapter of his book—that it was written under the direction of an angel. He described it; and his description would now exactly apply to the Book of Kells. But in those times there were many such books. We can hardly be surprised at Giraldus's legend; for whoever looks closely into some of the lovely pages of the Book of Kells—even in the photographic reproductions—will be inclined to wonder how any human head could have designed, or how any human hand could have drawn them.

These beautiful books were all written by Christian artists. We do not know if there was any attempt to ornament books in pagan times. But the pagan Irish, long before the introduction of Christianity, practised art of another kind—Metal-work—and attained great perfection in it. Those old artists exercised their skill in making and ornamenting shields; trumpets; swords with[Pg 96] their hilts and scabbards; chariots; bridles; brooches; gold gorgets or circlets for the neck; and so forth.

We can now judge of their handiwork for ourselves; for numerous beautiful specimens are preserved in our museums. The most remarkable are what are now commonly called 'Crescents,' of which we have many in the National Museum, in Dublin. These are broad circlets of pure gold to be worn round the neck, all covered over with ornamental designs. Both the general shape and the designs were produced by hammering with a mallet and punches on shaped solid moulds. The patterns and workmanship are astonishingly fine, showing extraordinary skill in manipulation: they are indeed so complicated and perfect that it is difficult to understand how they could have been produced by mere handwork, with hammers, punches, and moulds. Yet they could have been made in no other way.

We may see then that when St. Patrick arrived, in the fifth century, he found the art of working in metals already highly developed. We know that he kept, as part of his household, smiths, brasiers, goldsmiths, and other artists, who were constantly employed in making crosses; crosiers; chalices; bells; and such like.

[Pg 97]On the score of obtaining skilled workmen there was no difficulty, for he had plenty of pagan artists to choose from, who, on their conversion, turned their skill to Christian work, and found little difficulty in adapting their cunning fingers to new objects and to new forms of ornamentation. So the primitive pagan artistic metal work was continued on and improved in Christian times, and was brought to the highest perfection in the tenth and eleventh centuries. The ornamentation was generally like that used in manuscripts (p. 92).

Many of the beautiful objects made by those accomplished artists are now preserved in museums; some of them will bear comparison with the best works of the kind executed by artists of other countries; and a few might be found to bear the palm from all.

The three objects that are usually brought forward as examples of the best workmanship of the Irish Christian artists are the Cross of Cong, the Ardagh Chalice, and the Tara Brooch, all of which may be seen in the National Museum in Dublin: but there are many others in the same museum almost equally beautiful. These three will be found pretty fully described, with illustrations, in the two Social Histories of Ancient Ireland. The Tara Brooch was shown some years[Pg 98] ago in one of the great London exhibitions, and drew the eyes of all visitors. One English writer, who examined it and wrote an account of it, says that he found a difficulty in conceiving how any fingers could have made it, and that it looked more like the work of fairies than of a human artist.

CHAPTER XIII.
HOW THE ANCIENT IRISH PHYSICIANS WERE SKILLED IN MEDICINE.

Among most nations of old times there were great leeches or physicians, who were considered so skilful that the people believed they could cure wounds and ailments as if by magic. In some countries they became gods, as among the Greeks.

The ancient Irish people, too, had their mighty leech, a Dedannan named Dianket, who, as they believed, could heal all wounds and cure all diseases; so that he became the Irish God of Medicine. He had a son, Midac, and a daughter, Airmeda, who were both as good as himself; and at last Midac became so skilful that his father killed him in a fit of jealousy. And after a time there grew up from the young physician's grave[Pg 99] 365 herbs from the 365 joints and sinews and members of his body, each herb with mighty virtue to cure diseases of the part it grew from. His sister Airmeda plucked up these herbs, and carefully sorting them, wrapped them up in her mantle. But the jealous old Dianket came and mixed them all up, so that no one could distinguish them: and but for this—according to the legend—every physician would now be able to cure all diseases without delay, by selecting and applying the proper herbs.

Leaving these shadowy old-world stories, let us come down to later times, when we shall, as it were, tread on solid ground. We find in some authorities a tradition that in the second century before the Christian era, Josina, the ninth king of Scotland, was educated in Ireland by the Irish physicians, and that he afterwards wrote a treatise on the virtues and powers of herbs. Though we may not quite believe this tradition, it shows that the Irish medical doctors had a reputation abroad for great skill at a very early period.

Surgeons and doctors figure conspicuously in the old tales of the Red Branch Knights, and indeed in very many others, whether historical or romantic and fictitious: as well as in the strictly historical writings. A medical staff always[Pg 100] accompanied armies, each man having, slung from his shoulder, a bag full of herbs, ointments, bandages, and such other medical appliances as were used at the time. They followed in the rear of the army— each company under one head doctor; and at the end of each day's fighting—or during the fighting when possible—they came forward and applied their salves.

We are all now familiar with the humane practice of giving medical aid to the wounded after the battle, without distinction of friend or foe. The same practice was common in Ireland two thousand years ago. We read in one of the Tales, that when Kehern, a famous Ulster hero, returned from fighting, all covered with wounds, the Ulstermen sent a request to the Connaught camp—*i.e.*, the camp of the enemy—for physicians, as it happened that none of the Ulster leeches were just then at hand: and physicians were promptly despatched with the messenger.

A king or a great chief had always a physician as part of his household, to attend to the health of his family. The usual remuneration of these men was a residence and a tract of land in the neighbourhood, free of all rent and taxes, together with certain allowances: and the medical man might, if he chose, practise for fee outside the household.[Pg 101] Some of those in the service of great kings had castles, and lived in state like princes. Those not so attached lived on their fees, like many doctors of the present day: and the fees for the various operations or attendances were laid down in the Brehon Law.

Though medical doctors were looked up to with great respect, they had to be very careful in exercising their profession. A leech who through carelessness, or wilful neglect, or gross want of skill, failed to cure a wound, might be brought before a brehon or judge, and if the case was proved home against him, he had to pay the same fine to the patient as if he had inflicted the wound with his own hand, besides forfeiting his fee.

Medicine, as a profession, like Law, History, etc., often ran in families in Ireland, descending regularly from father to son; and several distinguished Irish families were distinguished leeches for generations, such as the O'Shiels, the O'Cassidys, the O'Hickeys, and the O'Lees.

Each medical family kept a book, which was handed down reverently from father to son, and in which was written, in Irish or Latin, all the medical knowledge derived either from other books or from the actual experience of the various members of the family; and many of these old[Pg 102] volumes, all in beautiful handwriting, are still preserved in Dublin and elsewhere. As showing the admirable spirit in which those good men studied and practised their profession, and how much they loved it, it is worth while to give a translation of the opening statement, a sort of preface, in the Irish language, written at the beginning of one of these books, nearly six hundred years ago:—

"May the good God have mercy on us all. I have here collected practical rules of medicine from several works, for the honour of God, for the benefit of the Irish people, for the instruction of my pupils, and for the love of my friends and of my kindred. I have translated many of them into Gaelic from Latin books, containing the lore of the great leeches of Greece and Rome. These are sweet and profitable things which have been often tested by us and by our instructors.

"I pray God to bless those doctors who will use this book; and I lay it as an injunction on their souls, that they extract knowledge from it not by any means sparingly, and that they do not neglect the practical rules herein contained. More especially I charge them that they do their duty devotedly in cases where they receive no payment on account of the poverty of their patients.

[Pg 103]"Let every physician, before he begins his treatment, offer up a secret prayer for the sick person, and implore the heavenly Father, the Physician and Balm-giver of all mankind, to prosper the work he is entering upon, and to save himself and his patient from failure."

There is good reason to believe that the noble and kindly sentiments here expressed were generally those of the physicians of the time; from which we may see that the old Irish medical doctors were quite as devoted to their profession, as eager for knowledge, and as anxious about their patients as those of the present day.

The fame of the Irish physicians reached the Continent. Even at a comparatively late time, about three hundred years ago, when medicine had been successfully studied and practised in Ireland for more than a thousand years, Van Helmont, a well-known and distinguished physician of Brussels, in a book written by him in Latin on medical subjects, praises the Irish doctors, and describes them correctly as follows:—

"In the household of every great lord in Ireland there is a physician who has a tract of land for his support, and who is appointed to his post, not on account of the great amount of learning he brings away in his head from colleges, but[Pg 104] because he is able to cure diseases. His knowledge of the healing art is derived from books left him by his forefathers, which describe very exactly the marks and signs by which the various diseases are known, and lay down the proper remedies for each. These remedies [which are mostly herbs], are all produced in that country. Accordingly, the Irish people are much better managed in sickness than the Italians, who have a physician in every village."

The Irish physicians carefully studied all the diseases known in their time, and had names for them—names belonging to the Irish language, and not borrowed from other countries or other languages. They investigated and noted down the qualities and effects of all curative herbs (which had Gaelic, as well as Latin, names); and they were accordingly well known throughout Europe for their knowledge and skill in medicinal botany.

There were Hospitals all over the country, some in connexion with monasteries, and managed by monks, some under the lay authorities; and one or more doctors with skilled nurses attended each hospital, whether lay or monastic. The Brehon Law laid down regulations for the lay hospitals:—for instance, that they should be kept clean, and[Pg 105] should have four open doors for ventilation, that a stream of clear water should run across the house through the middle of the floor, that the patients should not be put into beds forbidden by the physician, that noisy talkative persons should be kept away from them; and many other such like. There were no such regulations for the monastic hospitals, as being unnecessary. The provision about the open doors and the stream of water may be said to have anticipated by more than a thousand years the present open-air treatment of consumption. Those who had means were expected to pay for food, medicine, physician, and attendance: but the poor were received and treated free.

If a person wounded or injured another unlawfully, he was obliged to pay for "sick maintenance," i.e., the cost of maintaining the wounded person in a hospital till recovery or death; which payment included the fees of the physician and of one or more nurses.

It is pleasant to know that the Irish physicians of our time, who, it is generally agreed, are equal to those of any other country in the world, can look back with respect, and not without some feeling of pride, to their Irish predecessors of the times of old.

[Pg 106]
CHAPTER XIV.
HOW THEY BUILT AND ARRANGED THEIR HOUSES.

Before the introduction of Christianity, buildings of every kind in Ireland were generally round or oval. The quadrangular shape, which was used in the churches in the time of St. Patrick, came very slowly into use; and round structures finally disappeared only in the fourteenth or fifteenth century. But the round shape was not universal, even in the most ancient period. Look at the plan of Tara, at the beginning of this book, and you will see that the Banqueting Hall was quadrangular, the only building of this shape on the whole hill. And in this respect Tara may be said to represent the proportion for the whole of Ireland: that is to say, while the generality of buildings were oval or round, some—very much the fewer in number—were quadrangular, sometimes long in shape, sometimes square.

There were many centres of population, though they were never surrounded by walls; and the dwellings were detached and scattered a good deal—not closely packed as in modern towns. The dwelling-houses, as well indeed as the early[Pg 107] churches, were nearly always of wood, as that material was much the most easily procured. But although wood-building was general in Ireland before the twelfth century, it was not universal: for many stone churches, as we have seen, were erected from the time of the introduction of Christianity; and there were small stone houses from time immemorial.

The dwelling-houses were almost always constructed of Wickerwork. The wall was formed of long stout poles standing pretty near each other, with their ends fixed deep in the ground, the spaces between closed in with rods and twigs neatly and firmly interwoven; generally of hazel. The poles were peeled and polished smooth. The whole surface of the wickerwork was plastered on the outside, and made brilliantly white with lime, or occasionally striped in various colours; leaving the white poles exposed to view.

In many superior houses, and in churches, a better plan of building was adopted, by forming the wall with sawed planks instead of wickerwork. In the houses of the higher classes the doorposts and other special parts of the dwelling and furniture were often made of yew, carved, and ornamented with gold, silver, bronze, and gems.

[Pg 108]In the sunniest and pleasantest part of the homestead the women had a separate apartment or a separate house for themselves, called a 'Greenan' meaning a 'sunny apartment' or a summer-house; to which they retired whenever they pleased.

The roof was covered with straw, or rushes, or reeds, or with thin boards of oak, laid and fastened so as to overlap, like our slates and tiles. Occasionally churches were roofed with lead.

In great houses there were separate sleeping-rooms. But among the ordinary run of comfortable, well-to-do people, including many of the upper classes, the family commonly lived, ate, and slept in the one principal apartment, as was the case in the houses of the Anglo-Saxons, the English, the Germans, and the Scandinavians of the same period. But the sleeping-places and beds were shut in from view; for in at least the better class of houses in Ireland there were, ranged along the wall, little compartments or cubicles, each containing a bed, or sometimes more, for one or more persons, with its head to the wall. The wooden partitions enclosing the beds were not carried up to the roof; they were probably about eight or nine feet high, so that the several compartments were open at top.

[Pg 109]The homesteads had to be fenced in to protect them from robbers and wild animals. This was usually done by digging a deep circular trench, the clay from which was thrown up on the inside. This was shaped and faced; and thus was formed, all round, a high mound or dyke with a trench outside, and having one opening for a door or gate. Whenever water was at hand the trench was flooded as an additional security: and there was a bridge opposite the opening, which was raised, or closed in some way, at night. The houses of the Gauls were fenced round in a similar manner.

Numbers of these old circular forts still remain in every part of Ireland, but more in the south and west than elsewhere; many of them still very perfect: but of course the timber houses erected within them are all gone. Almost all are believed in popular superstition to be the haunts of fairies. They are still known by the old names—

lis, rath, brugh, múr, dún, moat, cashel, and *caher:* the cashels, múrs, and cahers being usually built of stone without mortar. The forts vary in size from 40 or 50 feet in diameter, through all intermediate stages up to 1,500 feet: the size of the homestead depending on the rank and means of the owner.

[Pg 110]Very often the flat middle space is raised to a higher level than the surrounding land, and sometimes there is a great mound in the centre, with a flat top, on which the strong wooden house of the chief stood. The outer defence, whether of clay, or stone, or timber, that surrounded the homestead was generally whitened with lime; and on the top all round, there was a hedge or strong palisade for additional security. Beside almost every homestead was a Kitchen Garden for table vegetables. And hard by were several enclosed spaces for various purposes, such as games and exercises, storing up the corn in stacks, securing the cattle at night, etc.

For greater security, dwellings were often constructed on artificial islands made with stakes, trees, and bushes, covered with earth and stones, in shallow lakes, or on small flat natural islands if they answered. These were called by the name *Crannoge*. Communication with the shore was carried on by means of a small boat, commonly dug out of one tree-trunk. The remains of these crannoges may still be seen in some of our small shallow lakes. In most of them old ferry-boats have been found, of which many specimens are now preserved in museums.

CHAPTER XV.
HOW THEY ATE, DRANK, FEASTED, AND ENTERTAINED.

Dinner, the principal meal of the day, was taken late in the afternoon; and there was commonly a light repast or luncheon, called 'Middle-meal,' between breakfast and dinner. It was the custom to have better food on Sundays and church festivals than on the other days.

Among the higher classes great care was taken to seat family and guests at table in the order of rank; and any departure from the established usage was sure to lead to quarrels. The king was always attended at banquets by his subordinate kings, and by other lords and chiefs. Those on his immediate right and left had to sit at a respectful distance. While King Cormac Mac Art sat at dinner, fifty military guards remained standing near him.

The manner of arranging the banquets at Tara was generally followed at other royal entertainments. The Banquet-hall here was a long building, with tables arranged along both side-walls.[Pg 112] Immediately over the tables were a number of hooks in the wall at regular intervals to hang the shields on. Just before the beginning of the feast all persons left the hall except three:—A *Shanachie* or historian: a marshal to regulate the order: and a trumpeter. The king and his subordinate kings having first taken their places at the head of the table, the professional ollaves sat down next them. Then the trumpeter blew the first blast, at which the shield-bearers of the lordly guests (for every chief and king had his shield-bearer or squire) came round the door and gave their masters' shields to the marshal, who, under the direction of the shanachie, hung them on the hooks according to rank, from the highest to the lowest. At the next blast the guests all walked in leisurely, each taking his seat under his own shield (which he knew by special marks).

Only one side of the tables was occupied, namely, the side next the wall: and in order to avoid crowding, the shields were hung at such a distance that when the guests were seated "no man of them would touch another." This arrangement at table according to rank was continued in Ireland and Scotland down to a recent period, as Scott often mentions in his[Pg 113] novels; and it continues still everywhere, though in a less strict form.

At all state banquets particular joints were reserved for certain chiefs, officials, and professional men, according to rank. A thigh was laid before a king, and also before an ollave poet; a haunch before a queen; a leg before a young lord; a head before a charioteer, and so on. A similar custom existed among the ancient Gauls and also among the Greeks. A remnant of this old custom lingered on in Scotland and Ireland down to a period within our own memory. Seventy years ago in some parts of Ireland, when a farmer killed a bullock or a pig, he always sent the head to the smith, so that at certain times of the year you might see the smith's kitchen garnished with forty or fifty heads hanging round the walls.

In the time of the Red Branch Knights, it was the custom to assign the choicest joint or animal of the whole banquet to the hero who was acknowledged by general consent to have performed the bravest and greatest exploit. This piece was called *curath-mir*, i.e., 'the hero's morsel or share'; and there were often keen contentions among the Red Branch heroes, and sometimes fights with bloodshed, for this coveted joint or piece. This usage, which prevailed among[Pg 114] the continental Celts in general, and which also existed among the Greeks, continued in Ireland to comparatively late times.

Tables were, as we have seen, used at the great feasts. But at ordinary meals, high tables, such as we have now, do not seem to have been in general use. There were small low tables, each used no doubt for two or more persons. Often there was a little table laid beside each person, on which his food was placed—the meat on a platter.

Forks are a late invention: of old the fingers were used at eating. In Ireland, as in England and other countries in those times, each person held his knife in the right hand, and used the fingers of the left instead of a fork. The Greeks and Romans had no forks at meals: they used the fingers only, and were supplied with water to wash their hands after eating.

As early as the eighth or ninth century the Irish of the higher classes used napkins at table, for which they had a native word *lambrat*, i.e., 'hand-cloth.' I suppose the chief use they made of it was to wipe the left-hand fingers; which was badly needed. It was the custom, both in monastic communities and in secular life, to take off the shoes or sandals when sitting down to[Pg 115] dinner; which was generally done by an attendant. The Romans we know had the same custom. The Irish did not sit up at dinner as we do now; but, like the Romans, they reclined on couches on which the feet also rested; and this was why the shoes were taken off.

In old times people were quite as fond of intoxicating drinks at dinners and banquets as they are now. They sometimes drank more than was good for them too: yet drunkenness was looked upon as reprehensible. At their feasts they often accompanied their carousing with music and singing. Besides plain water and milk, the chief drinks were Ale and Mead or metheglin, which were made at home; and Wine which was imported from France.

In great houses there were professional cooks, who, while engaged in their work, wore a linen apron round them from the hips down, and a flat linen cap on the head. But among ordinary families the women did the cooking.

Meat and fish were cooked by roasting, boiling, or broiling. A spit (*bir*), made of iron, was regarded as an important household implement. But the spits commonly used in roasting, as well as the skewers for trussing up the joint, were pointed hazel-rods, peeled and made smooth and[Pg 116] white. Meat, and even fish, while roasting, were often basted with honey or with a mixture of honey and salt.

In the house of every chief and of every brewy (see p. 119 below) there was at least one bronze Caldron for boiling meat. It was highly valued, as a most important article in the household; and it was looked upon as the special property of the chief or head of the house—much in the same way as his sword and shield. Everywhere we meet with passages reminding us of the great value set on these caldrons. One of them was regarded as a fit present for a king. The caldron was supposed to be kept in continual use, so that food might be always ready for guests whenever they happened to arrive. Many bronze caldrons have been found from time to time, and are now preserved in the National Museum, Dublin— several of beautiful workmanship.

In early ages kitchen utensils were everywhere regarded as important. The inventory of the jewels of the English King Edward III. gives a list of his frying-pans, gridirons, spits, etc. There is a curious provision in the Brehon Law that if any accident occurred to a bystander by the lifting of the joint out of the boiling caldron, the attendant was liable for damages unless he[Pg 117] gave the warning:—"Take care: here goes the fleshfork into the caldron!"

Milk was used both fresh and sour: butter was made in a small hand-churn; and cheese of various kinds was made from curds. There were water-mills and querns to grind corn, and sieves to separate the ground corn into meal and flour. The staple food of the great mass of the people was porridge, or, as it is now called in Ireland, stirabout, made of meal, generally oatmeal. It was eaten with honey, butter, or milk, as *kitchen* or condiment.

All the various kinds of meal and flour were baked into cakes or loaves of different shapes. Flour was usually mixed with water to make dough: but bread made of flour and milk was also much in use. Honey was often kneaded up with cakes as a delicacy: and occasionally the roe of a salmon was similarly used. Wheaten bread was considered the best, as at present: barley-bread was poor. Yeast, or barm, or leaven was used both in baking and in brewing.

The management of Bees was universally understood, and every comfortable householder kept hives in his garden. Wild bees, too, swarmed everywhere—much more plentifully than at present, on account of the extent of woodland.[Pg 118] Accordingly honey was very plentiful, and was used with all sorts of dishes. Often at meals each person had placed before him on the table a little dish, sometimes of silver, filled with honey; and each morsel whether of meat, fish, or bread was dipped into it before being conveyed to the mouth. Honey was the chief ingredient in the making of mead.

As the country abounded in forests, thickets, and brakes, the most common Fuel for domestic use was wood: but peat or turf was also much used, cut from a bank with a *slaan* or turf-spade as at present. Founders and other workers in metal used wood-charcoal, of which that made from birch-wood gave the greatest heat.

Flint and steel with tinder (or *spunk*) were used for striking and kindling fire. The whole kindling-gear—flint, steel, and tinder—was carried in the girdle-pocket, so as to be ready to hand; and accordingly, fire struck in this way was called *tinnĕ-crassa*, 'girdle-fire.'

For Light, dipped candles were used in the better class of houses. Poor people used dipped rushes, which gave a feeble light and burned out quickly. In the houses of the rich they used beeswax candles, as indeed we might expect from the great abundance of bees.

[Pg 119]Hospitality and generosity were virtues highly esteemed in ancient Ireland; in the old Irish Christian writings indeed they are everywhere praised and inculcated as religious duties; and in the secular literature they are equally prominent. The higher the rank of the person the more was expected from him, and a king should be hospitable without limit. There were all over the country Public Hostels for the free lodging and entertainment of travellers. At the head of each was an officer called a *Brewy* or *Beetagh*, a public hospitaller or hosteller, who was held in high honour.

In order to be at all times ready to receive visitors, a brewy was bound to have three kinds of meat cooked and ready to be served up to all who came; three kinds of raw meat ready for cooking; besides animals ready for killing. In one of the law tracts a brewy is quaintly described as "a man of three snouts":—viz. the snout of a live hog rooting in the fields; the snout of a dead hog on the hooks cooking; and the pointed snout of a plough: meaning that he had plenty of live animals and of meat cooked and uncooked, with a plough and all other tillage appliances.

There should be a number of open roads leading to the house of a brewy, so that it might[Pg 120] be readily accessible: and on each road a man was stationed to make sure that no traveller should pass by without calling to be entertained; besides which a light was to be kept burning on the lawn at night to guide travellers from a distance. To enable him to meet this great expense and to pay himself into the bargain, a brewy was allowed a great tract of land free.

Besides the hostels, there were the monasteries, too, where travellers were also boarded and lodged free for the time. And along with all this the people were kind and hospitable in their own houses to strangers and visitors. So we see that travellers were quite as well off then as now: indeed in one respect much better off: for whereas we have to pay a smart charge in an inn or hotel, there was in those times a hearty welcome and no charge at all.

The Irish missionaries carried this fine custom to the Continent in early ages, as they did many others: for they established free hostels in France and Germany, in places where there were no monasteries, chiefly for the use of pilgrims on their way to Rome.

[Pg 121]
CHAPTER XVI.
HOW THE PEOPLE DRESSED.

An oval face, broad above and narrow below, golden hair, fair skin, white, delicate, and well-formed hands with slender tapering fingers: these were considered as marking the type of beauty and of high family descent; they were the Marks of Aristocracy. To these natural advantages the people added by the usual artificial means. Among the higher classes the finger-nails were kept carefully cut and rounded. It was considered shameful for a man of position to have rough unkempt nails. Crimson-coloured finger-nails were greatly admired; and ladies sometimes dyed them this colour. Deirdrĕ, uttering a lament for the sons of Usna, says:—"I sleep no more, and I shall not crimson my nails; no joy shall ever again come upon my mind."

Ladies often dyed the eyebrows black with the juice of some sort of berry. We have already seen (p. 54) that the Irish missionary monks sometimes painted or dyed their eyelids black. An entry in Cormac's Glossary plainly indicates that[Pg 122] the blush of the cheeks was sometimes heightened by a colouring matter obtained from the alder tree: and the sprigs and berries of the elder were applied to the same purpose. Among Greek and Roman ladies the practice was very general of painting the cheeks, eyebrows, and other parts of the face.

Both men and women wore the hair long, and commonly flowing down on the back and shoulders. The hair was combed daily after a bath. The heroes of the Fena of Erin, before sitting down to their dinner after a hard day's hunting, always took a bath and carefully combed their long hair.

Among the higher classes in very early times great care was bestowed on the hair; its regulation constituted quite an art; and it was dressed up in several ways. Very often the long hair of men, as well as of women, was elaborately curled. Conall Kernach's hair, as described in the story of Da Derga, flowed down his back, and was done up in "hooks and plaits and swordlets." The accuracy of this and other similar descriptions is fully borne out by the most unquestionable authority of all, namely, the figures in the early illuminated manuscripts and on the shrines and high crosses of later ages. In nearly all the figures of the Book of Kells, for example (seventh or[Pg 123] eighth century), the hair is combed and dressed with the utmost care, so beautifully adjusted indeed that it could have been done only by skilled professional hairdressers, and must have occupied much time. Whether in case of men or women, it hangs down both behind and at the sides, and is commonly divided the whole way, as well as all over the head, into slender fillets or locks, which sometimes hang down to the eyes in front. I do not find mentioned anywhere that the Irish dyed their hair, as was the custom among the Greeks and Romans.

The men were as particular about the beard as about the hair. The fashion of wearing the beard varied. Sometimes it was considered becoming to have it long and forked, and gradually narrowed to two points below. Sometimes—as shown in many ancient figures—it falls down in a single mass; while in a few it is cut straight across at bottom not unlike Assyrian beards. Nearly all have a mustache, in most cases curled up and pointed at the ends as we often see now. In many the beard is carefully divided into slender twisted fillets, as described above for the hair. Kings and chiefs had barbers in their service to attend to all this. Razors were used made of bronze as hard as steel, as we know by finding[Pg 124] them mentioned in Irish documents as early as the eighth century; and many old bronze razors are now preserved in museums.

From what precedes it will be understood that combs were in general use with men as well as with women; and many specimens of combs are now found in the remains of ancient dwellings.

Bathing was very usual, at least among the upper classes, and baths and the use of baths are constantly mentioned in the old tales and other writings. In every public hostel, in every monastery, and in every high-class house, there was a bath, with its accompaniments. Soap was used both in bathing and washing.

Woollen and linen clothes formed the dress of the great mass of the people. Both were produced at home; and in chapter xix. the modes of manufacturing them will be mentioned. Silk and satin, which were of course imported, were much worn among the higher classes. The furs of animals, such as seals, otters, badgers, foxes, etc., were much used for capes and jackets, and for the edgings of various garments, so that skins of all the various kinds were valuable. They formed, too, an important item of everyday traffic, and they were also exported.

The ancient Irish loved bright colours. In this[Pg 125] respect they resembled many other nations of antiquity—as well indeed as of the present day; and they illustrated Ruskin's saying—"Whenever men are noble they love bright colour, and bright colour is given to them in sky, sea, flowers, and living creatures." The Irish love of colour expressed itself in all parts of their raiment; and we know that they well understood the art of dyeing. The several articles of dress on one person were usually coloured differently. Even the single outer cloak was often striped, spotted, or chequered in various colours. King Domnall, in the seventh century, on one occasion sent a many-coloured tunic to his foster-son Prince Congal: like Joseph's coat of many colours.

A very common article of dress was a large cloak, generally without sleeves, varying in length, but commonly covering the whole person from the shoulders down. The people also wore a tight-fitting coat with sleeves, something like our present frock-coat; but it was much shorter and without a collar, and it was kept tight by a belt round the waist. A short cape was often worn on the shoulders, sometimes carrying a hood to cover the head. The outer covering of the general run of the peasantry was just one loose sleeved coat or mantle, generally of frieze, which covered[Pg 126] them down to the ankles; and which they wore winter and summer. Women commonly wore a long loose cloak, with a hood, a fashion which is common at the present day. The over-garments were fastened by brooches, pins, buttons, girdles, strings, and loops, many of them beautifully made and ornamented.

The ancient Irish wore a trousers which was so tight-fitting as to show perfectly the shape of the limbs. When terminating below the ankles it was held down by a slender strap passing under the foot. Like other Irish garments it was generally striped or speckled in various colours. Leggings of cloth or of thin soft leather were used, and were laced on by strings tipped with white bronze, the bright metallic extremities falling down after lacing, so as to form pendant ornaments. A *kilt* was often worn, in which case the legs were left bare at the knees, with leggings below: for the kilt is of Irish origin, and was brought—like many other fashions—by the early colonists to Scotland, where it is still held on, while it has been long disused in Ireland.

Both men and women wore a garment of fine texture next the skin, commonly made of wool or linen, but sometimes of silk or satin, embroidered[Pg 127] with devices in gold or silver thread worked with the needle.

Girdles were commonly worn round the waist inside the outer loose mantle: those used by high-class people were often elaborately ornamented so as to be worth as much as from £40 to £100 of our present money. Garters were worn, partly for use, partly for ornament: often they were made of very expensive materials. Gloves were very common among all classes high and low, and were often highly ornamented.

The men wore a hat of a conical shape without a leaf; but among the peasantry, men, in their daily life, commonly went bare-headed, wearing the hair long behind so as to hang down on the back, and clipped short in front. Married women usually had the head covered either with a hood or with a long web of linen wreathed round and round in several folds. The veil was in constant use among the higher classes, and when not actually worn was usually carried, among other small articles, in a lady's ornamental hand-bag.

Shoes were often made of untanned hide stitched with thongs, with several layers for a sole. But there was a more shapely shoe, made of fully tanned leather, having serviceable sole and heel, and often ornamented with patterns stamped in.

[Pg 128]The Irish were excessively fond of personal ornaments, which among the higher classes were made of expensive materials, such as gold, silver, gems, white bronze, etc. They wore rings and bracelets of various shapes on the fingers (including the thumb), round the wrist and forearm, and even round the leg above the ankle. Necklaces were very common, from the cheapest kind up to those with the studs made of gold, pearls, and other gems, all of which materials were found native.

They had torques for the neck made of twisted gold bars; and the elaborate and immensely expensive crescents or gorgets have been already described (p. 96). There was a gold ornament—a kind of open ring with bosses or buttons on the ends—called *Bunnĕ-do-at*, worn on the breast: suspended from an ornamented button. Thin circular gold plates were also worn fastened on the breast: and as for brooches, they were of all shapes and sizes,

36

some plain, simple, and cheap, some of gold or other expensive material, of elaborate workmanship.

Pictures and full descriptions of all these ornaments will be found in either of the two Social Histories.

[Pg 129]
CHAPTER XVII.

HOW THEY FENCED IN AND TILLED THEIR LAND.

Ever since that remote time when legend and history begin to give us glimpses of the occupations of the inhabitants of this country, we find them engaged in Agriculture and Pasturage. For both of these purposes open land was necessary; and accordingly, people worked hard in old times to clear the land from wood. But there was always more pasturage than tillage.

In very early ages there was little need of fences, for the people were few and the land was mostly common property. But as the population increased it became more and more necessary to fence off the portions belonging to different individuals. The Brehon Law describes the several kinds of farm fences, some of which are still used; and it lays down strict rules regarding them.

Fences or merings of a more enduring kind were needed to bound off large territories or sub-kingdoms. There were several kinds of these territorial boundaries, some natural, some artificial, the most usual being rivers, roads, pillar-stones, and great ramparts of earth sometimes extending for miles.

[Pg 130]Manure—chiefly stable-manure—is often mentioned in the Brehon Laws. The laws also take account of several things that add to the value of land; such as a wood properly fenced in: a mine of copper or iron: the site of an old mill [with millrace and other accessories, rendering easy the erection of a new mill]: a road opening up communication: situation by the sea, by a river, or by a cooling-pond for cattle. The art of obtaining water by digging deeply into the ground was understood and practised.

Most of the native crops now in use were then known and cultivated: chief among them being corn of various kinds. Nearly all the agricultural implements now known were then used:—such as ploughs, sickles, spades and shovels, flails, rakes, clod-mallets, etc.

The chief farm animals were cows, pigs, sheep; and oxen, which were used for ploughing and for drawing waggons. Horses were not then so much used in farm-work as they are now. Pigs were kept in great droves at very little expense; for as forests abounded everywhere, the animals were simply turned out into the woods in care of a keeper, and fed on nuts, roots, and whatever else they could pick up.

Cows and sheep were very often grazed on[Pg 131] 'Commons,' i.e., tracts of grassy uncultivated land lying near a village—generally upland or mountain land—which belonged to the whole of the village or townland, but not to any particular individuals. These commons exist to this day near many villages, and are still used as in old times.

Women always did the milking, except of course in monasteries, where no women were employed, and the monks had to do all the work of the community.

CHAPTER XVIII.

HOW IRISH HANDICRAFTSMEN EXCELLED IN THEIR WORK.

All the chief materials for the work of the various crafts were produced at home. Of wood there was no stint: and there were mines of copper, iron, lead, and possibly of tin, which were worked with intelligence and success.

From the most remote times there were in Ireland professional architects or builders, as there were smiths, poets, historians, physicians, and druids; and we find them mentioned in our earliest literature. There were two main branches[Pg 132] of the builder's profession:—stone-building and wood-building. An ollave builder was supposed to be master of both.

The most distinguished ollave builder of a district was taken into the direct service of the king, and received from him a good yearly stipend: for which he was to oversee and have properly executed all the king's building and other structural works. In addition to this he was permitted to exercise his art for the general public for pay: and as he had a great name, and had plenty of time on hands, he usually made a large income.

The three chief metal-workers were the *Gobha* [gow], the *Caird*, and the *Saer*. The gobha was a smith—a blacksmith; the caird, a worker in brass, gold, and silver—a brasier, goldsmith, or silversmith; the saer, a carpenter or a mason—a worker in wood or stone.

We have already seen that the ancient Irish were very skilful in metallic art. Metallic compounds were carefully and successfully studied, copper commonly forming one of the ingredients. The most general alloy was Bronze, formed of copper and tin: but brass, a compound of copper and zinc, was also used. There were two kinds of bronze:—red bronze, used for spear-heads,[Pg 133] caldrons, etc.; and white bronze, which was much more expensive, and used for ornamental works of art—fine metal-work of all kinds.

The exquisite skill of the ancient Irish brasiers is best proved by the articles they made, of which hundreds are preserved in our museums. The gracefully-shaped spear-heads, which, in point of artistic excellence, are fully equal to any of those found in Greece, Rome, or Egypt, were cast in moulds: and we have not only the spear-heads themselves but many of the moulds, usually of stone. In one glass case in the National Museum there are more than forty moulds for bronze axes, spear-heads, arrow-heads, etc.: some looking as fresh as if they had been in use yesterday. The old cairds were equally accomplished in making articles of hammered bronze, of which the most characteristic and important are the great trumpets (page 87 above) and the beautifully-formed caldrons (page 116)—many of admirable workmanship—made of a number of bronze plates, hammered into shape and riveted together.

In old times in Ireland, blacksmiths were held in great estimation; and in the historical and legendary tales, we find smiths entertaining kings, princes, and chiefs, and entertained by them in turn. We know that Vulcan was a Grecian god;[Pg 134] and the ancient Irish had their smith-god, Goibniu, the Dedannan, who figures in many of the old romances.

The old Irish smith's anvil was something like the anvil of the present day, but not quite so large and heavy: it had the usual long snout, and was fixed firmly on a block. There were sledges and hand-hammers, pincers or tongs, and a water-trough. The bellows was very different from the present smith's bellows: it had two air-chambers of wood and leather lying side by side and communicating with the blowing-pipe. These were worked by a bellows-blower, who stood with his feet on the two upper boards, and pressed them down alternately, by which the two chambers were emptied in turn into the main pipe, so as to keep up a continuous blast. It should be remarked that in private houses they used a different sort of bellows, commonly called a 'blower,' which was held in the lap, and worked by turning a handle: this, by means of cog-wheels, caused a number of little fans in the inside to revolve rapidly, and thus to force a current through the pipe.

The fuel used by metal-workers was wood-charcoal. The smith's furnace was made of moist clay, specially prepared, a sort of fire-clay, which was renewed from time to time when[Pg 135] needed. This furnace surrounded and confined the fire on four sides, otherwise the light charcoal would be scattered by the blast of the bellows.

There was plenty to do for carpenters and other wood-workers, more indeed than for almost any other tradesmen, as the houses were then nearly all made of wood.

The yew-tree was formerly very abundant. Its wood was highly valued and used in making a great variety of articles: so that working in yew was regarded as one of the most important of trades. It required great skill and much training and practice: for yew is about the hardest and most difficult to work of all our native timber: and the cutting-tools must have been particularly fine in quality. Various domestic vessels were made from it, and it was used for doorposts and lintels and other prominent parts of houses, as well as for the posts, bars, and legs of beds and couches, always carved. Yew-carving accordingly gave much employment. There were also painters and metal-engravers; and here it is just as well to remark once for all, that the various articles of everyday life—hats, curraghs, shoes, book-covers, shields, chariots, leather, and so on, were made by special tradesmen (or women), all with their several suitable tools and instruments. The[Pg 136] makers of vessels of wood, metal, and clay were very numerous, and they were quite as skilful and dexterous as those of the present time. A thousand years ago the Irish coopers were able to make vessels of staves bound with hoops, like our tubs and churns, as water-tight and as serviceable as those made by the best coopers of our day.

The tools used by the various tradesmen are often mentioned in the Brehon Laws, from which we learn that there was as great a variety in Ireland then as there is now: but our limited space will only allow us to barely mention a few. There were saws, axes, hatchets, and hammers of various shapes and sizes; an adze for coopers and shield-makers; compasses for circles; planes both for flat surfaces and for moulding; lathes and potter's wheels for turning in wood and soft clay; chisels and gouges, awls, and augers. Besides the common whetstone they used a circular grindstone, which was turned on an axis by a cranked handle like those now in use.

Numerous stone structures erected in Christian times, but before the Anglo-Norman invasion, with lime-mortar, still remain all over the country, chiefly primitive churches and round towers. It is only necessary to point to the round towers to show the admirable skill and the delicate[Pg 137] perception of gracefulness of outline possessed by the ancient Irish builders. A similar remark might be made regarding many of the ancient churches.

Artificers of all kinds held a good position in society and were taken care of by the Brehon Law. Among the higher classes of craftsmen a builder of oratories or of ships was entitled to the same compensation for any injury inflicted on him in person, honour, or reputation, as the lowest rank of noble: and similar provisions are set forth in the law for craftsmen of a lower grade.

No individual tradesman was permitted to practise till his work had been in the first place examined at a meeting of chiefs and specially qualified ollaves, held either at Croghan or at Emain, where a number of craftsmen candidates always presented themselves. But besides this there was another precautionary regulation. In each district there was a head-craftsman of each trade, designated *sai-re-cérd* [see-re-caird], *i.e.*, "sage in handicraft." He presided over all those of his own craft in the district: and a workman who had passed the test of the examiners in Croghan or Emain had further to obtain the approval and sanction of his own head craftsman[Pg 138] before he was permitted to follow his trade in the district. It will be seen from all this that precautions were adopted to secure competency in handicrafts similar to those now adopted in the professions.

Young persons learned trades by apprenticeship, and commonly resided during the term in the houses of their masters. They generally gave a fee: but sometimes they were taught free or—as the law-tract expresses it—"for God's sake." When an apprentice paid a fee, the master was responsible for his misdeeds: otherwise not. The apprentice was bound to do all sorts of menial work—digging, reaping, feeding pigs, etc.—for his master, during apprenticeship.

CHAPTER XIX.
HOW THEY PREPARED AND MADE UP CLOTHING MATERIALS.

The wool was taken from the sheep with a shears having two blades and two handles, much the same as our present hedge-shears. After the shearing the whole work up to the finished cloth was done by women, except fulling, which was[Pg 139] regarded as men's work. The wool, after shearing, was sorted and scoured to remove the grease, and then carded into soft little rolls ready for spinning. Both wool and flax were spun with the distaff and spindle as in other countries; for the spinning-wheel was not invented till the fifteenth or sixteenth century.

The thread was woven in a hand-loom, nearly always by women in their own homes. Ladies of high rank practised weaving long ornamental scarfs as an accomplishment, which they did by means of a long thin lath—something like our crochet work—as the Greek ladies of old practised weaving ornamental webs. The woollen cloth was fulled or thickened by men who practised fulling as a distinct trade.

Our records show that linen was manufactured in Ireland from the earliest historic times. It was a very common article of dress, and was worked up and dyed in a great variety of forms and colours, and exported besides to foreign nations. So that the manufacture for which Ulster is famous at the present day is merely an energetic development of an industry whose history is lost in the twilight of antiquity.

The flax, after pulling, was tied up in sheaves and dried, after which it was put through various[Pg 140] stages of preparation much like those of the present day. After spinning, the thread was finally wound in balls ready for weaving.

The beautiful illumination of the Book of Kells, the Book of Mac Durnan, and numerous other old manuscripts, proves that the ancient Irish were very skilful in colours: and the art of dyeing was well understood. The dyestuffs were not imported: they were all produced at home, and were considered of great importance.

The people understood how to produce various shades by the mixture of different colours, and were acquainted with the use of mordants for fixing the dyes. One of these mordants, alum, is a native product, and was probably known in very early times. Dyeing was what we now call a cottage industry, *i.e.*, the work was always carried on in the house: as I saw it carried on in the homes of Munster more than half a century ago.

The cloth was dyed by being boiled with the several dyestuffs. The dyestuff for black was a sediment or deposit of an intense black found at the bottom of pools in bogs.

A crimson or bright-red colour was imparted by a plant which required good land, and was cultivated in beds like table-vegetables, requiring[Pg 141] great care. There were several stages of preparation; but the final dyestuff was a sort of meal or coarse flour of a reddish colour.

The stuff for dyeing blue was obtained from the woad-plant (called in Irish *glasheen*) after several stages of preparation, till it was made into cakes fit for use. A beautiful purple was produced from a sort of lichen growing on rocks, after careful preparation. A still more splendid purple was obtained from a little shellfish or cockle. This method of obtaining purple was practised also by the ancient Britons or Welsh; and by the same process was produced the celebrated Tyrian purple in still more distant ages.

For sewing, woollen thread was usually employed. Women sewed with a needle furnished with an eye as at present. From an early time needles were made of steel, but in primitive ages of bronze. In those days a steel or bronze needle was difficult to make; so that needles were very expensive: the price of an embroidering needle was an ounce of silver. The old Irish dressmakers were accomplished workers. The sewing on ancient articles of dress found from time to time is generally very neat and uniform: one writer describes the sewing on a fur cape found in a bog as "wonderfully beautiful and regular."

[Pg 142]Embroidery was also practised as a separate art or trade by women. An embroiderer kept for her work, among other materials, thread of various colours, as well as silver thread, and a special needle. The design or pattern to be embroidered was drawn and stamped beforehand, by a designer, on a piece of leather, which the embroiderer placed lying before her and imitated with her needle. This indicates the refinement and carefulness of the old Irish embroiderers. The art of stamping designs on leather, for other purposes as well as for embroidery, was carried to great perfection, as we know from the beautiful specimens of book-covers preserved in our museums.

Ladies of the highest rank practised needlework and embroidery as an accomplishment and recreation. For this purpose they spun ornamental thread, which, as well as needles, they constantly carried about in a little ornamented hand-bag.

The art of tanning leather—generally with oak-bark—was well understood in Ireland. By the process of tanning, the hide was thickened and hardened, as at present. Tanned leather was used for various purposes, one of the principal being as material for shoes; and we know that[Pg 143] curraghs or wicker-boats were often covered with leather. A jacket of hard, tough, tanned leather was sometimes worn in battle as a protecting corselet.

CHAPTER XX.

HOW THE IRISH TRAVELLED ON LAND AND WATER.

That the country was well provided with roads we know from our ancient literature, and from the general use of chariots. They were not indeed anything like our present hard, smooth roads, but constructed according to the knowledge and needs of the period, sometimes laid with wood and stone, sometimes not, but always open and level enough for car and horse traffic. There were five main roads leading from Tara through the country in different directions: and numerous roads—all with distinct names—are mentioned in the annals. Many of the old roads are still traceable: and some are in use at the present day, but so improved to meet modern requirements as to efface all marks of antiquity.

In old times the roads seem to have been very well looked after: and the regulations for making[Pg 144] and cleaning them, and keeping them in repair, are set forth with much detail in the Brehon Laws.

Rivers were usually crossed by bridges, which were made either of planks or of strong wickerwork supported by piles. Where there were no bridges people had to wade or drive across broad shallow fords: or to use a ferryboat if the stream was deep; or as a last resource to swim across.

The higher classes had chariots drawn by horses: usually one horse or a pair: but sometimes there were four. The chariot was commonly open: but some were covered over by an awning or hood of bright-coloured cloth, luxuriously fitted up, and ornamented with gold, silver, and feathers. The body of the chariot was made of wickerwork supported by an outer frame of strong wooden bars: and it was frequently ornamented with tin. The wheels were about four feet high, spoked, and shod round with iron. But no matter how carefully and beautifully it was constructed the Irish chariot, like those of the Greeks, Romans, and other ancient nations, was a springless jolting machine and made a great deal of noise. Two persons commonly rode in a chariot, the master and the charioteer. The general run of people used cars drawn by oxen.

[Pg 145]Horses were put to the same uses as at present:—riding, drawing chariots, racing; and more rarely ploughing, drawing carts, and as pack-animals. A bridle with a single rein was used in horse-riding. The rein was attached to a nose-band not at the side but at the top, and came to the hand of the rider over the animal's forehead, passing right between the eyes and ears, and being held in its place by a loop or ring in the face-band which ran across the horse's forehead. This single rein was used to restrain merely: it could not be used to guide. No spurs were used: the rider urged on and guided the horse with a rod having a hooked goad at the end. The ancient Irish—like the Britons, Gauls, and Romans—used no saddles: but there was usually a thick cloth between rider and horse. Chariot-drivers sat too far from the horse to make use of a horse-rod; so they used a two-rein bridle like ours.

Those who kept horses for riding were very fond of ornamenting their bridles and trappings with gold, silver, and enamel: so that the bridle alone was often worth from five or six cows up to eighteen or twenty.

The Irish used several kinds of boats, of which the commonest was the curragh, made of wickerwork woven round a frame of strong wattles, and[Pg 146] covered with hides which were stitched together with thongs. Boats of this kind are still used round the coasts, but tarred canvas is employed instead of skins, as being cheaper. Those used on rivers and lakes and on short coast voyages, were small and light and covered with a single skin. But those intended for rough seas and long voyages were made large and strong, with solid wooden decks and seats, and a mast, spars, and sails, so that they could be propelled by oars or sails, or both together. These were covered with two, or with three, hides, one outside another, and the hides were tanned so as to make them thick and hard, much the same as our thick leather. Some of these were large enough to hold fifty or sixty people. It should be remarked that wicker-boats were also used very generally in Britain, and occasionally on the coasts of some parts of the Continent.

The Irish had also ordinary wooden ships with sails and oars, and with sleeping-berths, like our small sailing vessels, and these they often used in very long voyages, either for trade or invasion. But for foreign expeditions their favourite vessel was the strong well-made curragh; and how suitable and safe these curraghs were is indicated by the fact that on one occasion Julius Cæsar ordered[Pg 147] a number of them to be made for use in some special expedition. Gildas, a British writer, tells us that whole armies of the Irish were often seen landing on the British shores from curraghs; and an ancient Irish writer says that during a certain military expedition the sea between Ireland and Scotland looked as if covered with a continuous bridge of curraghs.

The people of Ireland carried on considerable trade with England, Scotland, and the Continent. So constant was their communication with the Continent, that, as we are told by a great Roman writer, foreign merchants were, in those early days, better acquainted with the harbours of Ireland than with those of Britain.

The various articles mentioned in our records as brought from foreign lands to Ireland were imported to supplement the home produce; in which there was nothing more remarkable than our present importation of thousands of articles from foreign countries, all or most of which are also produced at home. The articles anciently imported were paid for in home commodities—skins and furs of various animals, wool and woollens, oatmeal, fish, salted hogs, etc.

[Pg 148]
CHAPTER XXI.
HOW THE PEOPLE HELD GREAT CONVENTIONS AND FAIRS; AND HOW THEY AMUSED THEMSELVES.

Public assemblies of several kinds and for various purposes were held all through Ireland; they were considered very important, and were looked forward to on the several occasions with great interest. Affairs of various kinds, some affecting the whole kingdom, some the particular province or district, were transacted at these meetings.

The laws were, when necessary, publicly recited to make the people familiar with them. There were councils or courts to consider and settle such matters as the claims of individuals to certain privileges; acts of tyranny by rich and powerful people on their weaker neighbours; disputes about boundaries; levying fines; imposing taxes for the construction and repair of roads; and such like. In fact the functions of these meetings of more than a thousand years ago were in many respects like those of our present county and district councils. In all the assemblies of whatever kind there were markets for the sale and purchase of commodities.

[Pg 149]Some meetings were established and convened chiefly for the transaction of serious business: but even at these there were sports and pastimes: in others the main object was the celebration of games: but advantage was taken of the occasions to discuss and settle important affairs, as will be described farther on.

The three great assemblies of Tara, Croghan, and Emain were not meetings for the general mass of the people, but conventions of delegates who represented the kingdoms and sub-kingdoms, i.e., the states in general of all Ireland, and who sat and deliberated under the presidency of the supreme monarch. The word Féis [faish] was generally applied to these three meetings.

The Féis of Tara, according to the old tradition, was founded by Ollam Fodla [Ollav-Fóla], who was king of Ireland seven or eight centuries before the Christian era. It was originally held every third year, at Samain, i.e., 1st November. The provincial kings, the minor kings and chiefs, and the most distinguished ollaves (doctors) of the learned professions attended. According to some authorities it lasted for a week, i.e., Samain day with three days before and three days after: but others say a month.

Each provincial king had a separate house for[Pg 150] himself and his retinue during the time; and there was one house for their queens, with private apartments for each, with her attendant ladies. There was still another house called Rélta na bh-filedh [Railtha-na-villa], the "Star of the poets," for the accommodation of the ollaves, where these learned men held their sittings. Every day the king of Ireland feasted the company in the great Banqueting Hall, which was large enough for a goodly company: for even in its present ruined state it is

42

759 feet long by 46 feet wide. The results of the deliberations were written in the national record called the Saltair of Tara. The conventions of Emain and Croghan were largely concerned with industrial affairs (see page 137 above).

The Aenach or fair was an assembly of the people of every grade without distinction: it was the most common kind of large public meeting, and its main object was the celebration of games, athletic exercises, sports and pastimes of all kinds. The most important of the Aenachs were those of Tailltenn, Tlachtga, and Ushnagh. The Fair of Tailltenn, now Teltown on the Blackwater, midway between Navan and Kells, was attended by people from the whole of Ireland, as well as from Scotland, and was the most celebrated of all[Pg 151] for its athletic games and sports: corresponding closely with the Olympic, Isthmian, and other games of Greece. It was held yearly on the 1st August, and on the days preceding and following. Marriages formed a special feature of this fair. All this is remembered in tradition to the present day: and the people of the place point out the spot where the marriages were performed, which they call 'Marriage Hollow.' The remains of several immense forts are still to be seen at Teltown, even larger than those at Tara, though not in such good preservation.

The meetings at Tlachtga and Ushnagh, which have already been mentioned, seem originally to have been mainly pagan religious celebrations: but there were also games, buying and selling, and conferences on local affairs.

At the Irish fairs, wherever held, all kinds of amusements were carried on; for the people loved games, sports, and fun of every kind. In order to make sure that there should be nothing to spoil sport, there was a very strict law against brawls, quarrelling, or fighting. Anyone who struck a blow or raised any disturbance was sure to be punished: and if it was a very bad case, he was put to death. So if there were any grudges between individuals, or families, or clans, they[Pg 152] had to be repressed during these meetings. The old Greeks had a law for their games exactly similar, which they called the "Sacred Armistice."

An Irish fair in those times was a lively and picturesque sight. The people were dressed in their best, and in great variety, for all, both men and women, loved bright colours; and from head to foot every individual wore articles of varied hues. Here you see a tall gentleman walking along with a scarlet cloak flowing loosely over a short jacket of purple, with perhaps a blue trousers and yellow headgear, while the next showed a colour arrangement wholly different; and the women vied with the men in variety of hues.

The people were bright and intelligent and much given to intellectual entertainments and amusements. They loved music and singing, and took delight in listening to poetry, history, and romantic stories; and accordingly, among the entertainments and art performances was the recitation of poems and tales of all the various kinds mentioned at p. 75 above, like the recitations of what were called Rhapsodists among the Greeks. For all of these there were sure to be special audiences who listened with delight to the fascinating lore of old times. Music always formed[Pg 153] a prominent part of the amusements: and there was no end of harpers, timpanists, pipers, fiddlers, and whistle-players.

In another part of the fair the people gave themselves up to uproarious fun, crowded round showmen, jugglers, and clowns with grotesque masks or painted faces, making hideous distortions, all roaring out their rough jests to the laughing crowd. There were also performers of horsemanship, who delighted their audiences with feats of activity and skill on horseback, such as we see in modern circuses.

In the open spaces round the fair-green there were chariot and horse races, which were sure to draw great multitudes of spectators. Indeed some fairs were held chiefly for races, like those at the Curragh of Kildare, which was as celebrated as a racecourse twelve hundred years ago as it is now.

Special portions of the fair-green were set apart for another very important function—buying and selling. There were markets for stock and horses, for provisions and clothes; and there you might also see foreign merchants from Continental countries, exhibiting their gold and silver articles, their silks and satins, and many strange curiosities: all for sale. Embroidering-women—all natives—showed[Pg 154] off their beautiful designs, and often kept doing their work in presence of the spectators. A special space was assigned for cooking, which must have been on an extensive scale to feed such multitudes.

At length the leaders gave the signal that the aenach was ended; and the people quietly dispersed to their homes.

Hunting was one of the favourite amusements of the Irish. Some wild animals were chased for sport, some for food, and some merely to extirpate them as being noxious; but whatever might be the motive, the chase was always keenly enjoyed. It is indeed quite refreshing to read in some of the tales a description of a hunt and of the immense delight the people took in the sport and all its joyous accompaniments. The hunters led the chase chiefly on foot, with different breeds of hunting-dogs, according to the animals to be chased. The principal kinds of game were deer, wild pigs, badgers, otters, and wolves; and hares and foxes were hunted with beagles for pure amusement. Pig-hunting was a favourite sport. Wolves were hunted down with the great Irish wolf-dogs, some of which were as big as a colt or an ass.

Wild animals were trapped as well as chased. There was an elaborate trap for deer, a deep[Pg 155] pitfall with a sharp spear at bottom pointing upwards, all covered over and concealed by a *brathlang* or light covering of brambles and sods. There was a special trap for each kind of animal—wolf, wild-hog, otter, and so forth. Birds were caught with nets and cribs: and indeed bird-catching was considered of such importance, that it was regulated by a special section of the Brehon Laws called 'Bird-net laws.'

Fish were caught, as at present, with nets, with spears either single or pronged, and with hook-and-line. Fishing-weirs on rivers were very common. A man who had land adjoining a stream had the right to construct a weir for his own use: but according to law, he could not dam the stream more than one-third across, so that the fish might have freedom to pass up or down to the weirs belonging to others.

Coursing was another amusement, as we find mentioned in our literature. The dogs were pitted against each other; and it was usual to see greyhounds, trained for this special purpose, exhibited for sale in markets, like cows, horses, and sheep.

Hurling or goaling has been a favourite game among the Irish from the earliest ages: played with a ball and a *caman* or hurley as at present.[Pg 156] In the latter part of the last century it declined somewhat in popularity; but now there is a vigorous attempt to revive it. Our modern cricket and hockey are only forms of the old game of *caman*.

In ancient Ireland chess-playing was a favourite pastime among the higher classes. Everywhere in the Tales we read of kings and chiefs amusing themselves with chess, and to be a good player was considered a necessary accomplishment of every man of high position. In every chief's house there was accordingly at least one set of chess appliances for the use of the family and guests; namely, a chequered chess-board, with chessmen and a bag to hold them, which was often made of woven brass wire.

From the most remote times in Ireland, kings kept fools, jesters, clowns, and jugglers in their courts, for amusement, like kings of England and other countries in much later times. In the Tales we constantly read of such persons and their sayings and doings. They wore funny-looking dresses; and they amused the people something in the same way as the court fools and buffoons of later times—by broad impudent remarks, jests, half witty, half absurd, and odd gestures and grimaces. King Conari's three[Pg 157] jesters were such surpassingly funny fellows that, as we are told in the story of Da Derga, no man could refrain from laughing at them, even though the dead body of his father or mother lay stretched out before him. Professional gleemen—commonly called *crossans*—travelled from place to place earning a livelihood by amusing the people like travelling showmen of the present day.

There were hand-jugglers, who performed wonderful tricks of slight-of-hand. King Conari's head juggler and his trick of throwing up balls and other small articles, catching them one by one as they came down, and throwing them up again, are well described in the old tale of Da Derga:—"He had clasps of gold in his ears; and wore a speckled white cloak. He had nine [short] swords, nine [small] silvery shields, and nine balls of gold. [Taking up a certain number of them] he flung them up one by one, and not one of them does he let fall to the ground, and there is but one of them at any one time in his hand. Like the buzzing-whirl of bees on a beautiful day was their motion in passing one another."

CHAPTER XXII.
HOW THE CHARACTER OF THE OLD IRISH PEOPLE SHOWED ITSELF IN VARIOUS CIRCUMSTANCES AND ON VARIOUS OCCASIONS.

Some of the modes of salutation and of showing respect practised by the ancient Irish indicate much gentleness and refinement of feeling. When a distinguished visitor arrived it was usual to stand up as a mark of respect. Giving a kiss, or more generally three kisses, on the cheek, was a very usual form of respectful and affectionate salutation: it was indeed the most general of all. When St. Columba approached the assembly at Drum-ketta, "King Domnall rose immediately before him, and bade him welcome, and kissed his cheek, and set him down in his own place."

A very pleasing way of showing respect and affection, which we often find noticed, was laying the head gently on the person's bosom. When Erc, King Concobar's grandson, came to him, "he placed his head on the breast of his grandfather." Sometimes persons bent the head and went on one knee to salute a superior.

[Pg 159]Although there were no such institutions in ancient Ireland as pawn-offices, pledging articles as security for a temporary loan and its interest, was common enough. The practice was such a general feature of society that the Brehon Law stepped in to prevent abuses, just as our law now contains provisions to safeguard poor people from being wronged in their dealings with pawn-offices. A person might pledge any movable article—a horse, a brooch, a mantle, etc.—and the person holding the pledge might put it to its proper use while it remained with him. He was obliged to return it on receiving a day's notice, provided the borrower tendered the sum borrowed, with its interest: and if he failed to do so he was liable to fine. Borrowing or lending, on pledge, was a very common transaction among neighbours; and it was not looked upon as in any sense a thing to be ashamed of, as pawning articles is at the present day.

There were distinct terms for all the parts of these transactions—a loan for kindness merely, a loan for interest, a loan in general: and interest was designated by two distinct words. The existence in ancient Ireland of the practice of pledging and lending for interest, the designation of the several functions by different terms, and the recognition[Pg 160] of all by the Brehon Law, may be classed, among numerous other customs and institutions noticed throughout this book, as indicating a very advanced stage of civilisation. At what an early period this stage—of lending for interest—was reached may be seen from the fact that it is mentioned in an Irish gloss of twelve hundred years ago.

Old age was greatly honoured, and provision was made for the maintenance of old persons who were not able to support themselves. As to old persons who had no means, the duty of maintaining them fell of course on the children; and a son or daughter who was able to support parents but who evaded the duty was punished. If an old person who had no children became destitute the tribe was bound to take care of him. A usual plan was to send him (or her) to live with some family willing to undertake the duty, who had an allowance from the tribe for the cost of support.

In some cases destitute persons dependent on the tribe, who did not choose to live with a strange family, but preferred to have their own little house, received what we now call outdoor relief. There was a special officer whose business it was to look after them: or, in the words of the law tract, to "oversee the wretched and the poor," and[Pg 161] make sure that they received the proper allowance: like the relieving officer of our present poor laws. He was paid for this duty; and the law specially warned him not to take offence at the abuse he was likely to receive from the poor cross peevish old people he had in charge.

Care was taken that the separate little house in which a destitute old person lived should be a fit and proper one; and its dimensions and furniture, as well as the dimensions of the little kitchen-garden, are set forth in the law. The law also specifies three items of maintenance—food, milk, and attendance; and it adds that the old person was to have a bath at regular intervals, and his head was to be washed every Saturday.

From the arrangements here described it will be seen that there was a kindly spirit in the provisions for old age and destitution, and that the most important features of our modern poor-laws were anticipated in Ireland a thousand years ago.

"A thing of beauty is a joy for ever." So says the English poet, Keats, in his poem of Endymion, and he enumerates various natural features and artificial creations as things of beauty; among many others, the sun, the moon, "trees old and new," clear rills, "the mid-forest brake," "all[Pg 162] lovely tales that we have heard or read." If he had been in Ireland in old times, he would have come across delightful proofs of the truth of his saying everywhere among the people. They loved and had an intense appreciation of all things of beauty, whether natural or artificial; and they were remarkable for their close observation of the natural features of the world around them.

We know all this from their poetry, their tales, and their writings in general, which strongly reflect this pleasing aspect of their character. Everywhere we meet with passages in which are noticed, with loving admiration, not only those features mentioned by Keats, but many others, such as the boom and clash of the waves, the cry of the sea-birds, the murmur of the wind among the trees, the howling of the storm, the sad desolation of the landscape in winter, the ever-varying beauty of Irish clouds, the cry of the hounds in full career among the glens, the beauty of the native music, tender, sad, or joyous, and so forth in endless variety.

The few examples that follow here, as the reader will at once perceive, exhibit vividly this very fine and very attractive characteristic.

The singing of birds had a special charm for the old Irish people. Comgan, a poet of the seventh[Pg 163] century, standing on the great rath of Knockgraffon in Tipperary—one of the old Munster royal residences—which was in his time surrounded with woods, uttered the following verse:—

"This great rath on which I stand
Wherein is a little well with a bright silver drinking-cup:
Sweet was the voice of the wood of blackbirds
Round this rath of King Fiacha."

Among the examples of metre given in an old Irish treatise on prosody is the following verse, selected merely for a grammatical purpose:—

"The bird that calls within the sallow-tree,
Beautiful his beak and clear his voice;
The tip of the bill of the glossy jet-black bird is a lovely yellow;
The note that the merle warbles is a trilling lay."

It would be hard to find a more striking or a prettier conception of the power of music in the shape of a bird-song, than the account of Queen Blanid's three cows with their three little birds which used to sing to them during milking. These cows were always milked into a caldron, but submitted reluctantly and gave little milk till the birds came to their usual perch—on the cows' ears—and sang for them: then they gave their milk freely till the caldron was filled. This corresponds with the effect of the milking-songs described at p. 89. (See also for bird-songs, p. 83.)

[Pg 164]Many students of our ancient literature have noticed these characteristics of the old Irish and their writings. "Another poem," writes Mr. Alfred Nutt, "strikes a note which remains dominant throughout the entire range of Ossianic Literature: the note of keen and vivid feeling for certain natural conditions. It is a brief description of winter:—

"A tale here for you: oxen lowing: winter snowing: summer passed away: wind from the north, high and cold: low the sun and short his course: wildly tossing the wave of the sea. The fern burns deep red. Men wrap themselves closely: the wild goose raises her wonted cry: cold seizes the wing of the bird: 'tis the season of ice: sad my tale."

In a certain plain, simple prose narrative in one of our old books, where there is not the least effort at fine writing, it is related how, in the noon of a summer day, a little child fell over a cliff into the sea. The mother ran down shrieking expecting he was dashed to pieces: but she found him quite safe "sitting in the trough of the sea"—to quote the lovely words of the old writer—"playing with the waves. For the waves would reach up to him and laugh round him; and he was laughing at the waves, and putting the palm of his hand to the foam of the crest, and he used to lick it like the foam of new milk."

[Pg 165]In the Life of St. Columkille it is stated that, while residing in Iona, he wrote a poem in Irish, a tender reminiscence of his beloved native land, in which he expresses himself in this manner:—

St. Columkille's Remembrance of Erin.

"How delightful to be on Ben-Edar before embarking on the foam-white sea; how pleasant to row one's little curragh round it, to look upward at its bare steep border, and to hear the waves dashing against its rocky cliffs.

"A grey eye looks back towards Erin; a grey eye full of tears

"While I traverse Alban of the ravens, I think on my little oak grove in Derry. If the tributes and the riches of Alban were mine, from the centre to the uttermost borders, I would prefer to them all one little house in Derry. The reason I love Derry is for its quietness, for its purity, for its crowds of white angels.

"How sweet it is to think of Durrow: how delightful would it be to hear the music of the breeze rustling through its groves.

"Plentiful is the fruit in the Western Island—beloved Erin of many waterfalls: plentiful her noble groves of oak. Many are her kings and princes; sweet-voiced her clerics; her birds warble joyously in the woods: gentle are her youths; wise her seniors; comely and graceful her women, of spotless virtue; illustrious her men, of noble aspect.

"There is a grey eye that fills with tears when it looks back towards Erin. While I stand on the oaken deck of my bark I stretch my vision westwards over the briny sea towards Erin."

Even the place-names scattered over the country—names that remain in hundreds to this day—bear testimony to this pleasing feature of the Irish character: for we have numerous places still called[Pg 166] by names with such significations as "delightful wood," "silvery stream," "cluster of nuts" (for a hazel wood), "prattling rivulet," "crystal well," "the recess of the bird-warbling," "melodious little hill," "the fragrant bush-cluster," and so forth in endless variety.[7]

There is a very old legend that Ailill Inbanna, king of Connaught in the sixth century, earned heaven by his noble self-sacrifice in order to save his people. A bitter war was waged between him and the two princes Donall and Fergus, sons of the king of Ireland, till at last a decisive battle was fought between them at a place called Cúil-Conari, in the present county Mayo, in which Ailill was defeated. And at the end of the day, when he and his army were in full retreat, the king, sitting in his chariot in the midst of the flying multitude, said to his charioteer:—"Cast thine eyes back, I pray thee, and tell me if there is much killing of my people, and if the slayers are near us." The charioteer did so, and said:—"The slaughter that is made on thy people is intolerable." Then said the king:—"Not their[Pg 167]own guilt, but my pride and unrighteousness it is that they are suffering for. Turn now the chariot and let me face the pursuers; for as their enmity is against me only, if I am slain it will be the redemption of many." The chariot was accordingly turned round, and the king plunged amidst his foemen and was slain; on which the pursuit and slaughter ceased. That man, says the old legend, by giving up his life, in his repentance, to save his people, attained to the Lord's peace.

In the old Irish Canon Law, there was a merciful provision to save the family of a dead man from destitution if he died in debt; namely, that certain specified valuable articles—such as a cow, a horse, a garment, a bed, etc.—belonged to the family, and could not be claimed by a creditor.

The yellow plague wrought dreadful havoc in Ireland—and indeed desolated all Europe—in the seventh century. In Ireland at least it appears to have attacked adults more than children, so that everywhere through the country numbers of little children, whose mothers and fathers had been carried off, were left helpless and starving. At this same time lived Ultan,[Pg 168] the kindly bishop of Ardbraccan in Meath. It wrung his heart to witness

47

these piteous scenes of human suffering all round him; and he took steps, so far as he was able, to relieve and save the little children. He collected all the orphan babes he could find, and brought them to his monastery; and procuring a great number of cows' teats, and filling them with milk, he put them into the children's mouths with his own hands, and thus contrived to feed the little creatures. The number increased daily, so that at last he had as many as 150; and as he was not able to do all the work himself, he had to call in others to assist him in his noble labour of love.

It is proper to remark here that we find other examples in history of the use of a cow's teat for milk-feeding, and that in Russia infants are often fed in this way.

All this is remembered to St. Ultan down to the present day; for he is often mentioned in old Irish histories, almost always with a remark something like this:—"Little children are always playing round Ultan of Ardbraccan."

It would be difficult to find an instance where charity is presented in greater beauty and tenderness than it is in this simple story of the good bishop Ultan.